DEDICATION

For Faith, Felix, Oskar and Posey.

CONTENTS

Acknowledgments i

1 Introduction   Pg 1
2 A Brief History of Engagement Rings   Pg 7
3 Budgeting   Pg 11
4 What's Important?   Pg 16
5 Getting Her Involved   Pg 22
6 Going It Along   Pg 27
7 The Setting   Pg 34
8 Picking the Band   Pg 45
9 Sizing   Pg 51
10 Diamonds   Pg 54
11 Blood diamonds   Pg 76
12 Does It Need To Be A Diamond?   Pg 78
13 Where To Buy   Pg 93
14 Making Your Money Go Further   Pg 99
15 Closing The Deal   Pg 115
16 Insurance   Pg 126
17 Cheat Sheet   Pg 130
18 How I Did   Pg 135
19 Resources Round-up   Pg 139
   Ring Size Table   Pg 141
   References   Pg 143

ACKNOWLEDGMENTS

I'd like to thank:

Dave Walker for giving me the original idea for the book when I was on a totally different, and probably terrible course, (I'm not sure how much I would have added to the world's understanding of the menopause had I gone through with my plans to write a book on it).

Ben Crompton for reading the first draft and telling me when my attempts at jokes were terrible. Pied Piper!

Rory Kinsella for doing a great job of editing the book and ensuring that the phrase 'tie the knot' appears in the book only a bearable number of times.

Sionen Adijans for designing the front cover(s) and being a massive help with all things graphical.

Melissa Beale for keeping me right on all things jewellery and jewellers.

And of course Faith for agreeing to marry me, for inspiring this book and for being the best friend, and now wife, that I could have ever asked for.

1. INTRODUCTION

Absolutely freezing, we huddled under the blankets stolen from our hotel room. As we peered out into the uninspiring gloom, dew dripped from our noses, pooling into a snotty mess on the pilfered bedware. Behind us a noisy Filipino family conducted a raucous photo session – their jolly banter a contrast to our laboured chat as we struggled to make the best of a bad situation.

After 20 minutes, with buttocks cramping from the cold, unforgiving rocks, we decided that we'd had enough – it was time to retreat to the sanctuary of the rental car and head back to the hotel.

Disappointed but not defeated, I stowed the ring back in my backpack and we started the long trudge back to the carpark. So there it went – another opportunity to pop the question gone. But I had been carrying the ring around for months already, so what difference would a couple more weeks make?

This proposing lark was proving to be just as difficult as buying the ring in the first place.

The Plan

Proposing at sunrise on top of a volcano in Hawaii had seemed like a good idea when I was planning it back home in Australia. As the golden tendrils of sunlight arced over the horizon, I would stand proud atop the still-smoking caldera. Dropping to one knee, the light would refract through the diamond ring like a Pink Floyd album cover, bathing us in a dazzling rainbow. Speaking confidently yet tenderly, I would reduce my lady-friend to a quivering mess with the beauty of my oration. She would instantly say yes, bystanders would break into song, majestically-bosomed native women would present us with flower leis and the whole affair would end up as YouTube sensation.

That would be the easy bit. I'd already put the hard work, time and a few pay cheques into the most challenging part – finding the perfect engagement ring. The proposal would be child's play, right? Hmm...

So who am I?

I'm a 30ish English chap currently living in Sydney, Australia. After meeting Faith, my now fiancée, in Canada, we lived in London for five years before fleeing the drizzle and the impending economic meltdown to the land of sizzling barbecues, sun-kissed beaches and sunburnt skin (for me anyway).

Aside from the usual English hobbies of drinking beer and playing football badly, I spend the rest of my time working in marketing and trying to ingratiate myself into the Australian beach culture by failing miserably at surfing and cremating meat on the barbecue.

It might be a bit geeky, but I'm not afraid to admit that I love to learn. I love to educate myself on the world's most important issues but also find great pleasure in reading about the most niche and seemingly irrelevant interests. When I was younger, this meant constant library fines and worn out torch batteries as I read under the bed covers at night. Now it's a requirement for 24/7 internet access and hundreds of tabs open at any one time, filling my brain with both useful and completely useless information.

So when I decided to pop the question, I initially turned to the web to find out as much as I could. I'd suffered through enough rom-coms to know that a diamond was expected and the bigger the better. But I quickly realised that, for what was going to be a significant investment for me, there was very little information to help me make an informed decision.

Sure, there was some info about diamonds on jewellers' websites, but apart from that it was pretty thin on the ground. After reading a couple of blog posts and some threads written by women on bridal forums I had pretty much exhausted everything that the web could teach me about how to go about buying an engagement ring.

I talked to friends who had already proposed to get an idea of how they went about the process. What I quickly found was that many of them had jumped in without really knowing what they were doing, and had since found that they should have chosen a more suitable ring for their fiancée, or could have got a better deal on the ring that they did go with.

I decided to cast my net wider to see if I could find an authoritative and unbiased source on the subject. Amazon was happy to offer me hundreds of rings to choose from, but could only offer me one book. I snapped it up and read it as soon as it arrived. It was written by a middle-aged couple and was really, really dry and dull - full of way too much technical information that I didn't really need to know, but no advice on where to buy or how to get the most for my money.

So I realised that I would have to do some research myself – talking to as many real life people as possible until I felt that I was in a position to make an informed decision.

In June 2013 I travelled back to the UK from Australia via a stop-off in New York. This gave me the opportunity to compare rings over three continents. I spoke to mothers, grandmothers and my great-grandfather to see how things were done in their day. I found a couple of tame jewellers who were happy to give me the inside info on the jewellery industry over a coffee and I spoke to a gemologist friend-of-the-family who gave it to me straight on what does and doesn't matter with precious stones. And I researched other skills that I thought could be useful and applied to the purchase of an engagement ring.

What I found out was that choosing an engagement ring is difficult. There's a bewildering minefield of expectations, societal norms, jargon and conflicting information to negotiate.

What's this all about then?

The ring you buy is not only a significant financial investment; it's also a symbol of commitment for the most important relationship in your life.

From the moment you ask the question until your wedding day and beyond, your better half is going to be showing off her ring to anyone and everyone – friends, family, old ladies on the 149 bus – the lot. This book is going to help you get her a ring that she will love and be proud to show off – one that will earn approving nods from her mum and bus-riding-grannies alike. I'm also going to let you into a few secrets on how you can save a few shekels in the process and make your hard-earned cash go as far as possible.

Firstly, we'll look at a (very) brief history of engagement rings. As a manly man with many hairs on your chest, you probably don't care much about the history of jewellery, but it's interesting to see how our views on engagement rings have been formed and how recently this happened.

We'll then look at whether you should include your girlfriend in the search for the ring. It's a big decision and she will, hopefully, only ever get one engagement ring, so seeking her input may be the best way to ensure that she gets a ring she loves.

Following that decision, we'll look at the different options for rings themselves – from diamonds to other gemstones, silver bands to gold, platinum and beyond. Stones other than diamonds are increasingly popular and can make for a more interesting and unusual engagement ring.

However, diamonds are widely accepted as the standard engagement ring, and with that in mind, I'll talk you through what you need to know, going past just the '4 Cs' of cut, colour, clarity and carat that you will find on most jewellers' websites.

Once we've decided on the style of ring, we'll look at where to buy – from big name jewellers to back-alley pawn shops, from second-hand online deals through eBay to custom-made rings to your precise specifications.

I'll guide you through how to get the best price, what to watch out for and give you a crash course in negotiation: a skill that will serve you well beyond just haggling over the ring.

The aim of this book it to give you all the information that you really need to know to make a well informed decision on buying a ring - stripping out anything else that clouds the issue. This isn't intended to be a definitive guide to diamond buying - there are much longer, much more boring books about that. Instead, by the time you've finished reading you'll be ready to buy a ring that is going to wow your missus and make her friends jealous, all while saving you some beer tokens so that you can celebrate the big event.

Right, let's crack on.

2. A BRIEF HISTORY OF ENGAGEMENT RINGS

Although cavemen may have given their shiniest rock to the cavelady they'd just bashed over the head and dragged home to claim as their own, the first record of the giving of a physical symbol of betrothal is in Ancient Egypt, around 2000BC. Circles were used in the time of Tut to symbolise the eternal cycle of life, while the space inside it represented gateways. (And quite possibly ladies' front-bottoms too.)

This idea spread across the Mediterranean, with rings also given in Ancient Greece and Rome, where the tradition of placing the token on the fourth finger of the left hand began. Ancient Greeks believed that finger contained a vein that led straight to the heart. Roman brides were usually given two rings, a gold one which she wore in public, and one made of iron which she could wear at home while making Roman sandwiches and doing a bit of Roman dusting.

After all of these empires crumbled like Steve Guttenberg's post-Police Academy career, the idea of giving a physical symbol of betrothal disappears from the historical record, until around the 14th century when gold 'posie rings' were swapped by lovers.

But the person to blame for the rise of the diamond engagement ring is Archduke Maximilian of Austria, who gave the first well-documented diamond engagement ring to Mary of Burgundy in 1477. This set a trend among those who could afford it, although until diamonds were discovered in South Africa in 1870, they continued to be a rare commodity and only available to the very wealthiest.

As production and supply increased, prices decreased, but it was only as recently as the 1930s that diamond rings became the default choice for most engagements, as a result of some clever marketing.

A diamond is forever

De Beers is an international mining company that once controlled 90% of the world's diamond trade,[1] although this stranglehold has loosened in the last 20 years. In the 1930s, De Beers realised that diamonds were becoming increasingly common as mines opened up and that, as the stones became commoditised, their lack of intrinsic value would result in a reduction in prices. To counter this, De Beers needed to increase the perceived value of diamonds, and they did this by directly linking the size and quality of a diamond to a person's love for another.

In 1938, De Beers first ran what is often cited as the most successful ad campaign in history. Yes, even more effective than the Budweiser 'wassup' ads that embarrassing dads still quote to this day.

The brief for the advertising agency was "to create a situation where almost every person pledging marriage feels compelled to acquire a diamond engagement ring".

The first campaign used the tagline, "A diamond is forever" – cleverly tying the tough physical properties of a shiny bit of rock with the idea of a permanent commitment. Obviously the tagline was successful - it has entered everyday language. The ad agency also started lending diamonds to Hollywood stars to wear on-screen and at the Oscars, spreading the propaganda through the distribution of those films.[2]

Variations on this ad campaign have been running ever since and its success and the demand it generated, combined with De Beers regulating the supply of diamonds and keeping it artificially low, has ensured that prices have stayed high ever since.

After establishing diamonds as the one true symbol of lasting commitment, De Beers needed to convince men that they should spend a good whack of their hard-earned moola on one. In a campaign in the 1980s they came up with another line that still helps dictate the amount that men expect to spend on a ring: "Isn't two months' salary a small price to pay for something that lasts forever?"

The idea that diamonds are the one true symbol of love, commitment and betrothal has well and truly taken hold. Some men put off proposing until they have enough money for a diamond that they feel reflects the intensity of their love – all because of a 70-year-old ad campaign.

De Beers isn't the only devilishly clever company out there who has managed to change behaviour through marketing though. There are many other examples, like Coca-Cola popularising the idea that Santa Claus wears red by giving him their brand colours in a 1931 ad campaign[3] or Nike inventing the concept of jogging as a leisure activity.

The point of all this is to explain that, although the practice of giving a ring as a symbol of betrothal is an ancient one, the idea that it needs to be a diamond is not. Diamonds aren't rare or even particularly special – they're only expensive because De Beers has had such a firm grip on both supply and demand. If you would like to buck the norm and choose a different stone, you can and should do so and I'll talk you through your other options in Chapter 12. However, before you make any big decisions, it's a good idea to have a good think about what you can stretch to and what your ladyfriend is going to be expecting.

3. BUDGETING

Buying an engagement ring is a significant investment. I don't own a house and my cars have always been bangers, so the ring I chose was by far the most expensive thing I'd ever bought. But how do you decide how much to spend?

In the last chapter we learnt that the two, or even three, months' salary rule was a recent idea and not something you should worry about. However, as it turns out, the average ring price does work out to be roughly two months salary, after tax. The stats are similar across all Western countries, but in 2013, the average salary in the US was $49,000,[4] while the average price of engagement ring was around $5,300.[5]

In this chapter I'll talk you through some of the things I thought about when deciding how much to spend. I'll also let you know what you can get for your money and then later in the book we'll look at what you can do to make your money go further.

Setting a budget that's right for you

The most important thing with budget is to decide how much is right for your situation, and your beliefs.

I've got 100% Scottish blood running through my veins,

so I'm always looking for a bargain and keen to get as much value for money as possible. I'm a keen discount coupon collector and always take a packed lunch to work to avoid spending money on store-bought food.

At the same time, I'm not afraid to invest in quality. I've got a couple of expensive pushbikes and not even under the pain of nipple-clamp torture would I tell my other half how much they cost. I like to spend money on good quality clothes that will last, rather than disposable stuff from the high street. So I was happy to spend a decent chunk of change on a quality ring because it is something we will keep forever.

Different people have different attitudes and spending habits though. I have some friends who buy a new car every other year and think nothing of splashing $1,000 on a Dior handbag. But then there are others who will only shop in thrift stores, not because they want to cultivate a shabby hipster vibe, but because they just can't face spending their money on new clothes.

What's important is to think about yourself and the value that you, and your girlfriend, place on material things.

For some, a flash diamond will be a symbol of just how big their love is, while for others a simple token of commitment is all they need.

A good way to look at it is to fast-forward a year and think about what you would feel comfortable having paid. If you think that you'll have pangs of regret and break into cold sweats at having spent so much, then revise your budget down. In the end, it needs to be an amount that you're comfortable with, rather than going with what you think is expected.

Borrowing to pay for the ring

Although many people have tightened their belts following the credit crunch, a lot still rely on credit cards, especially for big purchases. Whether you stick your engagement ring on plastic is your call, but I would recommend you borrow only as much as you can honestly afford.

Feeling stressed about repayments or hiding how you paid for the ring from your partner could spoil the golden period of the engagement. Weddings are expensive enough and you don't want to go into the planning process already in debt from the engagement ring.

For me, saving for a ring was a gradual process, putting away a little at a time for a couple of years while we also saved towards a house deposit. This meant I was especially careful when choosing the ring as it was my money I was spending, rather than the bank's.

Top-level guide to ring prices

You might already have a rough idea of how much you want to spend, but if you haven't started looking at rings yet, you may not know how much a ring actually costs. At the beginning of this chapter, I gave you the average figure for a diamond engagement ring in the US, $5,300, but what do you get for this and what if you want to spend more, or less?

There are a huge number of factors that affect the price of an engagement ring, so at this stage I'll only give you a very top-level guide. We'll look at this in much more detail in Chapter 14: Making Your Money Go Further.

Around $5,000 will get you a high quality diamond of around 0.8 carats, or a 1 carat diamond with some compromises. Often a 1 carat diamond in this range will have issues with colour or cut, which can affect how much they sparkle. Choosing a stone smaller than 1 carat will mean that you have more budget to spend on some of the other characteristics that make up a quality diamond – you'll find out more about those later.

Spending a little more, say $7,000, will get you a quality 1 carat diamond in a good setting, possibly with some small sides stones too.

Dipping below the average – between $2,500 and $3,500 – and you should get a high quality diamond of about 0.5 carats. Although you can get 1 carat weight of diamonds at this price, it would be made up of several smaller stones instead of one whopper on the middle.

Under $2,500 with diamonds and you'll have to compromise on the setting – choosing a cheaper metal for the band. Below $1,000, the diamonds will be less than 0.5 carats with quality issues that affect their sparkle. If this is your budget it would be worth looking at an alternative to a diamond – another semi-precious gem.

Chapter 14 is where we'll look at how you can get the most value for your budget, but hopefully this top-level info is useful for you as you start thinking about ballpark figures for how much you are going to spend and what type of ring you will be able to buy.

In conclusion

The one thing that you need to take away from this chapter is that the amount that you spend on an engagement ring needs to be an amount that you are comfortable with. Don't succumb to pressure to conform or to spend a certain amount – you want to be able to enjoy the engagement without sweating about making repayments on the ring.

4 WHAT'S IMPORTANT?

When looking at engagement rings there is a dizzying array of options to consider, and it's hard to know what's most important. Will your girl˙ expect a Tiffany's box? Does it need to be a diamond? And does it have to be a particular size? Will she be upset if you don't spend a certain amount of money.

The table overleaf shows the outcome of a survey of over 2,700 men and women by theknot.com. They were asked to rank in order of importance eight key factors of engagement rings. It makes for pretty interesting reading, especially because there are some clear differences in what women want and what guys think women want.

As with all survey results, you'll need to filter it through the lens of your own knowledge about yourself and your other half, but there are some interesting things to note.

Rank in order of importance:

Grooms		Brides
Stone Quality	1	Style / Setting
Style / Setting	2	Stone Cut / Shape
Stone Cut / Shape	3	Stone Quality
Price / Value	4	Metal
Stone Size	5	Price / Value
Metal	6	Stone Size
Retailer	7	Retailer
Designer	8	Designer

Here's what I take out of this:

Designer comes lowest for both men and women

Unlike with clothes where a designer may have a signature style, silhouette or just a whopping great logo printed all over it, with engagement rings the designer is much less obvious. Many of the most popular rings are classic styles that are unchanged since the early 20th Century and any innovation in design often ends of becoming a trend, which is then copied by lots of ring makers.

The exception to the 'the designer doesn't matter' rule is if you want a custom ring. Here, the choice of designer is vital - you want to ensure that you are working with someone who has the technical skills to produce what you are looking for, but also that you get on with to ensure that you have a good working relationship with them.

Retailer is second lowest for both men and women

Equally, it's interesting to see that the retailer is given the second-lowest level of importance for both men and women.

There are of course a few big name jewellers that sell engagement rings – these will vary from country to country, but the most famous international retailer is probably Tiffany's.

As with all premium brands, jewellers can leverage the goodwill that surrounds them to charge a higher-than-market price. The brand increases the perceived value, without adding any real value.

A Volkswagen Golf has the same underpinnings as an Audi A3. They have the same chassis, they share engines, but people are willing to pay a premium for the Audi over the Golf not because it's a better car, but because of the association with the Audi brand.

It's easy to tell an Audi from a VW – the extra money invested has a noticeable result: a different body and badge which elicit different emotions. They may even get you a little more acceptance in the country club car park. But with engagement rings, the difference between a branded ring and an unbranded one is much less noticeable. It's almost impossible to tell the difference unless you are a trained jeweller.

So don't spend your money on a branded ring where the difference will be lost as soon as it is taken out of the box. Instead, invest in the attributes of the ring that people will actually notice and value.

Groom's number one is stone quality

Like a lot of guys I know, I obsess over details when I'm doing research before buying something. I want to know that my mountain bike has the most suspension travel in its class, my phone screen has the most pixels and my food mixer has enough power to blend an iPad (it can and there's a video on YouTube to prove it).[6] We like to go for the 'best of breed' of everything.

Really though, these requirements are excessive. Although I have six inches of suspension travel, I'm lame enough at mountain biking that four would do. It doesn't help me stay on my bike any more than my friends. My phone has a 2k screen which means that I can watch HD movies on the toilet, but it's way beyond what I need for Facebook and grainy YouTube videos of squirrels on waterskis. And though it's useful to know that I can destroy all the household electronics I please, all I really use the blender for is making short work of the odd kumquat.

With each of these, I could have saved cash by settling for the 'best of need', rather than 'best of breed'. Things that take care of what I need, without excessive capabilities and the hefty price tags they bring.

With engagement rings, it's important not to get carried away with stone quality, especially when the differences between gradings can't be seen by naked eye, even by a trained jeweller. We'll look at this in much more detail later on in the book.

I'm not suggesting you opt for a cheaper or 'worse' ring, but you should consider spending some of the budget that could go on stone quality on some other things instead – such as size of rock or quality of band.

Bride's number one is Style/Setting

Brides rated the style and setting of a ring as their top priority – the thing they care about most, so it's the one thing you need to make sure you get right.

If there is one main objective for this eBook, it's to help you find a style and setting that your girl will love.

Style and setting incorporate a range of factors:

- What stone or stones are used
- The way they are set on the band
- Any design that is incorporated into the wedding band itself

To make sure that you get the setting right, in upcoming chapters we're going to look at whether you should get your girlfriend involved in the buying process, how you can go about finding out what she wants without her ever knowing what you're up to and also an in-depth look at ring settings.

Stone Cut/Shape

Stone cut and shape rated highly for both men and women. Along with the style and setting, they are one of the most obvious visual markers of an engagement ring. There are a wide range of cuts and shapes, all of which go in and out of fashion. This means that certain cuts demand a premium over others, even if the diamond itself is the same size and quality.

This means that if your girl is looking for an unusual or older cut found in a vintage ring, you may be able to pick up a bargain.

Metal

Generally, women prefer either gold or silver-coloured jewellery – seldom both. Unfortunately, even in this enlightened age segregation by colour is still very much alive in most jewellery boxes. In Chapter 8, we'll look at how to choose the right metal for your ring.

And in conclusion

There are clear differences between men and women's priorities, and also some similarities too. Retailer and designer are both bottom of the pile for both, that's clear.

But men put much more focus on stone quality - it's their number one, while women only rank it number three. As the ring is really for her, make sure you take note of this and focus on the setting - it's the most important thing to get right.

5 GETTING HER INVOLVED

A common question that guys struggle with is whether they should involve their girlfriend in the process of choosing the ring. The thought of blowing her mind with a surprise proposal featuring the perfect sparkler is enticing, but this carries with it the very real risk that you could choose a ring that she doesn't like.

There's no right or wrong answer to this question and there are three ways to tackle it:

1. Going all out secret squirrel

2. Discussing options with her before shopping yourself

3. Taking her with you and shopping together

According to another survey by theknot.com, the split between the options is very even:[7]

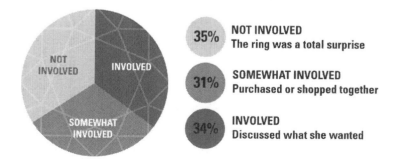

35% NOT INVOLVED
The ring was a total surprise

31% SOMEWHAT INVOLVED
Purchased or shopped together

34% INVOLVED
Discussed what she wanted

Before you decide which is the right route for you though, take a minute to think about if the roles were reversed and you were letting your better half make a significant decision for you. Whether it's choosing your car or picking your fantasy football team, would you trust her to make the exact right choice with no supervision?

This chapter will talk you through some of the pros and cons of each of the options and help you decide which to go for.

Going it alone

Pros:

- Keeps the proposal a surprise
- Extra brownie points if you get it right
- More romantic

Cons:

- You could balls it up and buy a ring she hates

Should consider if:

- You're extremely confident about your lady's taste.

Would you buy a pair of shoes for her without checking whether she'll like them? If not, it's maybe not the best idea to risk so much on something she will wear for the rest of her life.

If this is the route that you're taking, we'll look at how you can go it alone and find a ring that your girl will love, without her knowing anything about it in the next chapter.

She's somewhat involved (you discuss what she wants)

Pros:

- Gives you an idea of the style of ring she likes
- A less stressful process for you
- Allows you to keep the final price a secret

Cons:

- Lose some of the surprise of the proposal
- She may have expensive tastes and high expectations and ask for more than you can afford

Should consider if:

You are unsure what she would like but have discussed marriage so she at least knows it's coming. It allows you to retain some of the surprise – she won't know when you've bought it, what it looks like or when you'll pop the question.

She's completely involved (you go shopping together)

Pros:

- You are sure to choose a ring she likes
- She will feel empowered

Cons:

- It takes the surprise out of it
- She'll know how much you're spending
- The shop assistant is likely to show her nicer, more expensive rings, straining your budget
- Haggling with her in the shop may make you look cheap

Should consider if:

Not just for those guys whose girlfriends wear the pants in their relationship, if your other half has very specific taste or if you just have no idea at all what she'd like, then taking her along to choose a ring will ensure that you get a ring that she loves.

The choice is yours

The decision on which route to take is up to you. Most of us aren't brilliant at being romantic, but buying a ring and surprising your girlfriend is a once in a lifetime opportunity to show how thoughtful you can be.

I was confident I could pick a ring that Faith would love. I'd bought her enough jewellery in the past to know what she liked and after eight years together, she'd even started wearing some of it.

However, the jeweller I spoke to said she'd had more men coming in with their girlfriends to look at rings together, although guys usually made the actual purchase on their own. The decision really is yours – and one you'll have to make depending on the dynamics of your own relationship.

The Get Out Clause

There is, however, one way that you can get your girlfriend involved in the purchase and knock her socks off with a surprise proposal.

By buying just a stone on its own, you can drop to one knee with a box and something shiny, but still get your lady-friend involved in the part of the ring choice process that is most important to her: selecting the setting.

And, to make sure that none of the magic is lost in the proposal, some jewellers will mount the stone in a temporary mock-setting, so you can still slip it onto her finger when she says yes.

For me, this is the best of both worlds: you can research and buy the stone that fits within your budget and plan a surprise proposal, while she will be able to choose the ring that she has always imagined receiving.

6. GOING IT ALONE

You may have already decided to strike out on your own, and for that I salute you. If you're still wondering whether it's right for you, whether it's possible, or even if it's sensible, this chapter will help you decide.

In this section, I'll talk through a few of the ways I subtly did the research to find a ring Faith would love. I was cunning as a fox that had been appointed Professor of Cunning at Harvard University. If you follow these tips, you too will be able to get a solid idea of the ring that she wants without her ever knowing.

Listening out

This one is key – not just when shopping for engagement rings, but for presents, where to go to dinner and even just for whether you should leave the toilet seat down a bit more. If your other half ever drops anything casually into conversation about a preference, a liking, something that she would someday maybe like to do, then know this: it wasn't casual.

Remember these things, take note and, heck, actually write a note so you remember to do something about it later.

This isn't being a sucker, it's saving you a lot of head-scratching when it comes to buying presents and will earn you huge brownie points when you have apparently read her mind and given her something she always wanted. As well as scars, chicks dig thoughtfulness.

If your girl has ever uttered a word about engagement rings, remember two things:

1. She's thinking about them and expecting one soon

2. That thing she just said? She expects you to take into account when buying one

You might not have written it down at the time but have a think, scratch your noggin and see whether you can remember her mentioning anything about engagement rings – either good or bad.

For me, when I searched my booze-addled brain, I had a vague recollection of Faith mentioning a diamond at some point, so this was my first clue in forming an idea of what she was after.

Reactions

It's a time-honoured tradition for newly-engaged women to flash their rocks to anyone and everyone, and there's no doubt that she will have had a few dangled in front of her. Tradition also dictates that she both ooohs and ahhhs appreciatively.

However, just because she makes encouraging noises within earshot of her rock-toting friend, it doesn't mean that she likes their ring.

If you're with her when she's shown a ring, offer up an opinion straight after. It doesn't matter what – you can say you loved it or hated it – the aim is to get a view back from her to give you guidance. In fact, offering up the opposite opinion to the one you expect her to have can be the best option. If you think the ring you've been shown would be perfect, say you hate it – it'll throw her off the scent and will ensure she gives you her opinion.

With me, we had a lot of friends get engaged in the year before I proposed, which gave me plenty of opportunities to listen for what she loved and what made her throw up a little in her mouth. Mixed colours on the band and multiple diamonds were out, a solitaire and a silver-coloured band were in. I was getting somewhere.

Check out existing jewellery

The colour and style of jewellery your girlfriend currently wears is one of the biggest indicators of what you should look at, for a couple of reasons.

Generally, women wear either gold or silver jewellery – seldom both. So your first job is to determine whether your girl usually wears gold or silver, as this will be the colour of engagement ring band you should buy.

You may already know from having bought her jewellery in the past. If she mixes it up and wears both, find out which she wears more – her engagement and wedding rings will be worn every day so need to complement the jewellery she usually wears.

If she wears gold, you'll have to choose between yellow gold, rose gold or 'old gold'.

If she prefers silver-coloured jewellery then your options are white gold or platinum – the most popular metal for engagement rings at the moment.

Aside from the colour of the band, the other thing her

existing jewellery can tell you is the general style of ring you should consider. Does she sport big, flashy jewellery – like she has a Studio 54 decoration hanging from each earlobe? If so, it's a safe bet she'll expect a flashy ring too.

But if she prefers understated jewellery, her engagement ring should follow suit and be simple but beautiful.

Personality

As well as the style and blinginess of her existing jewellery, her personality provides a huge indicator about what sort of ring she would love.

If she's an extrovert and will want to show off her ring to everyone she meets, she's going to want something big and sparkly.

More understated personalities are often reflected in someone's personal style. If she's quieter, a simpler ring may work out better.

Style

'You are what you wear', said someone, at some point, probably. And whether we like it or not, the clothes we choose, the car we drive and the way we decorate our houses are indicators of our ideas and even our personalities.

If your girl is into sleek design, with an apartment full of minimalist furniture, then the ring you choose should also be minimalist and simple.

Maybe she loves markets and bringing home antique furniture. If so, look at a reproduction of an art deco design, or go for a vintage ring.

If she dresses like she's in Mad Men then go for

something classic and timeless.

Perhaps she's a girly girl, with fabrics draped above her four-poster bed and wants to be Ariel from The Little Mermaid when she grows up. Look for something imaginative and elaborate, with art nouveau swirls.

Web research

I'm sure most men are aware of the benefits of clearing their browser history, but women usually have less need to do so. If you think your girl is looking at rings online, you can search her internet history on all the major browsers. Click 'show full history' and then run a search for 'engagement' to see if she's been doing some research of her own.

Online stalking

Sure, Facebook is good for finding bikini pictures of girls you went to school with to see if they're still hot, but Pinterest is where it's at for ring research stalking.

Many girls with Pinterest accounts will have a board dedicated to jewellery, or even to weddings. Some of my single girl friends have even got a fully stocked Pinterest board with their wedding decorations planned out. Which may go some way to explain why they're still single. But nevertheless – if your girlfriend does have a Pinterest account, have a look and you may find great clues.

One thing you may have to contend with is the 'private' Pinterest board, which hides selected boards from public view. The only way around this is to fire up her laptop when she's not looking and check it out directly - risky but potentially very rewarding.

The jewellery store mission

If you haven't had a chance to gauge a reaction from a show-and-tell session, then take matters into your own hands and conduct a covert op to get the primary intel you need.

Your mission, should you choose to accept it, is to venture deep behind enemy lines and take your girl into a jewellery store – into the very mouth of the beast.

Sounds risky, I know, but as any successful covert operative knows, the key to success is misdirection. Here's how it should go down.

Tell her you want to go shopping to check out some shoes – maybe something you wouldn't normally go for – those Vibram FiveFingers barefoot shoes you've heard such good things about? She'll want to come to give an opinion because she's the one who'll be seen with you, so won't want your feet to look like a gibbon's for the next six month

When you're in the shopping centre, casually drop into a jewellers to check out some watches. You've always promised yourself a decent watch and you're thinking about finally treating yourself. While you're looking at the Omegas (hey, good enough for James Bond) keep an eye on what your girl is doing. Odds are she'll have sidled over to the rings to have a good nosey about.

Make a mental note of what she's looking at and say something to prompt a reaction. Make it understated like, "That's a nice one," and gauge her reaction. Go back to the watches and leave without looking at the rings again. Mission accomplished.

I did this and it confirmed the type of ring that she was looking for, as well as narrowing down the cut of diamond to a square shape. This helped me massively when I was actually buying the ring, without Faith knowing that I was actually looking for one.

Ask her friends

'Three people can keep a secret if two of them are dead.'

Not a quote from the Hell's Angels handbook, but from Benjamin Franklin, one of America's not-as-friendly-as-I-thought Founding Fathers.[8]

The final idea here is not for everyone. It's a sure way to find an answer, but also the riskiest of the lot.

Have a think about whether there are any of your girlfriend's friends you could trust to keep it quiet. It's not a malicious secret, in fact it's one that if she breaks your trust will affect her relationship with your girlfriend rather than yours.

If there is a mutual friend, let her know you're trusting her and ask whether your girl has dropped any hints, or talked about what she wants.

A good way to make sure this stays secret is to stress to the friend that she is the only one you're asking and insist it remains a surprise.

Bringing it all together

If you've followed all these hints, or even some of them, you should be on your way to having an idea of what your girl wants. I nailed it down to the type of stone, metal and shape of stone without my missus knowing I was the least bit interested in engagement rings. And once I had those locked down, it was just a case of choosing the ring that had all the characteristics that I was looking for and worked within my budget.

7. THE SETTING

A ring's setting is the way that the stones are placed on the band. It's the ring's format and style and the defining characteristic of what a ring looks like. Setting is rated as number one on women's importance list, so it feels right that when getting into the nitty gritty of choosing a ring, I should talk about this first.

If you'd been planning to go it completely alone with the ring, don't be afraid of changing your mind and getting your other half involved after reading this chapter. I was lucky to have picked up enough hints to know my girl wanted a solitaire, but you might not be so fortunate.

I'll talk you through the most common settings, with pros and cons for each.

Solitaire

A solitaire setting has a single main stone in the centre of the ring – usually a round brilliant or a princess cut (you'll find out what those mean in Chapter 10). It's a simple setting which can keep the cost of the band and setting down, but because there are no side stones to support the main one, the centre stone is out there flapping in the wind and has to do the impressing on its own.

Solitaires are held in place with either four or six prongs. Having four allows the most light to enter the stone, which lets it to sparkle to the best of its ability. Six prongs, sometimes called the Tiffany setting because it was first produced by Tiffany & Co., holds the stone more securely but doesn't allow quite as much light in.

Bezel

A bezel setting has a metal rim that surrounds the sides of the stone and extends just above it. This is a secure setting and its low profile means it's suitable for women with active lifestyles - it won't get snagged on anything and the bezel will protect the stone.

It's also suitable for softer stones, as the bezel around the rim of the stone adds a layer of protection and can help prevent the centre stone from becoming chipped. With more metal than a solitaire, it can be slightly more expensive.

Pavé

Pavé is a ring 'paved' with diamonds — lots of small diamonds covering the whole ring, sometimes even the underside of the band. The advantage here is the bling you can get for not too much money. The small diamonds are relatively inexpensive but the effect is impressive.

It's a good option to support a smaller centre stone, although the cost of the increase in complexity and the number of supporting stones can match the reduction from the smaller centre stone. One way to reduce the budget is to go for a 'half pavé', where only the top of the band has stones.

Halo

A halo setting has a ring of smaller stones (the halo..) surrounding one large central stone. The halo stones can either be the same as the central stone, or you can mix it up with another colour. Halo settings will make a centre stone look bigger, which is great if you are going to go with a smaller centre stone.

Three stone

Three stone rings are sometimes called 'past, present and future' rings, with the stones said to represent the past, present and future of your relationship.

The advantage of a three stone setting for you is that you can get a higher carat weight of diamond for a greatly reduced price. For example, three 1/3 of a carat stones on a ring is much cheaper than a one carat solitaire.

The side stones don't need to be the same shape or even the same stone as the centre. Again, a great solution if you don't want to go with a whopping rock in centre.

Side Stone

Side stone settings go a step further than three stone settings and can be set up in a variety of ways, but they all have multiple stones flanking a central stone.

They're another good way of increasing the weight of the stones and ensuring that the main one doesn't have to impress on its own. The sizes and quality of the stones make a big difference to the price here, but you can get high quality precious gem side stones for surprisingly little money.

Channel

Channelling means that small stones have been included in a 'channel' in the band of a ring. It can be added to any ring to give it a bit of extra pizazz. It's often added to solitaires to give extra sparkle and works wonders if you can't stretch to a large centre stone.

Watch out: Total Diamond Weight

One thing to watch for with all of the settings with multiple stones is retailers trying to pull the wool over your eyes by quoting the 'Total Diamond Weight'. A ring with a TDW of 1.5 carats may only have a centre stone of 0.7 carats, with the remainder made up of the other, smaller stones, and should be significantly less expensive than a ring with a centre stone of 1.5 carats.

So, if you're looking at a ring with several stones, make sure you get clarity on both the TDW and the size of the centre stone.

Vintage

You may want to go vintage to avoid worries about blood diamonds, or because you think it will match your girlfriend's style. Vintage is a broad subset, but consists mainly of the following:

Victorian

Victorian rings (1830s - 1900) are rare because of their age, but if you do find one then they'll often have a large central stone supported by several smaller stones, a bit like a modern 'halo setting'. The settings themselves are often very intricate, with engravings of scrolls etc.

Diamonds were not as common then as they are today, so other stones were commonly used, like sapphires, rubies, emeralds, and pearls. All of these stones are much less hard than diamonds, so when looking at a ring that is well over 100 years old, you really need to do it in person to ensure that there is no damage to these softer stones.

Edwardian

Edwardian engagement rings (early 1900s) are very ornate, with the typical ring setting aiming to replicate the look of delicate lace. Many Edwardian engagement rings are platinum, which is good because it holds up so well to use. Diamonds, particularly in the 'rose cut' were popular for use in Edwardian engagement rings, but again it was before diamonds were widely available, so often less expensive stones were used. Sapphires, black opals and aquamarines were popular choices for the centre stone.

Art deco

Probably the most popular type of vintage ring are those from the art deco period (1920s - 1940s). Although there are no hard and fast rules on what makes something art deco, there are some principles that all design from that period sticks to. While Edwardian engagement rings were decorative, swirly and ultra-feminine, art deco is all about strong geometric shapes and symmetry.

One thing that did remain consistent from the Edwardian era was the use of platinum. Although gold and sometimes silver were used, it was the ultra-modern-for-the-time platinum that was favoured by those who could afford it.

Vintage ring watch-outs

One thing to note is that stone cutting technology has moved on a lot since these rings were created, so they may not have the quality of cut and sparkle of newer rings.

Also, ideas of perfection have changed. While white is now considered the optimum colour for diamonds, in the past green, yellow or rose tinted stones were preferred.

Lastly, although you may find a vintage ring that you love, it may not be able to be resized to fit your intended's finger. While rings can be sized up or down one or two sizes, with a vintage ring you are starting from a set point - the size of the previous owner's finger. And if this is drastically different from the size of your girlfriend's finger, it will be very difficult, and probably pretty expensive, to make it work.

Finding a setting that works

One thing to consider when choosing a setting is what will look best on your ladyfriend's fingers.

Some things to think about are:

- Women with long, slim fingers can get away with most of the styles listed

- Delicate settings can get lost on large hands, making the hands look bigger and the ring smaller (not good)

- Wide bands make fingers look shorter

- Big chunky settings such as the pavé can look oversized on a small hand

- An elongated centre stone, such as a marquise or oval (see Chapter 10) can make short fingers look longer

- If your girl has an active lifestyle, a ring that sits up above the band, like a pronged solitaire, can get snagged on clothes or equipment

Don't be afraid to ask

Setting really is one thing that you need to get right, so if you were previously planning to go it alone but are now not sure, there's no shame playing it safe and consulting your girlfriend. Alternatively, if you have an idea of what you think that you're going to go for, try the jewellery shop trick from the previous chapter to check whether you're right.

And remember, you can always invoke the get-out clause

and choose the setting with your new fiancée after you have proposed with just a stone. This can be an absolute life-saver as you still get to retain the all-important surprise factor but also ensure that she gets a setting that she absolutely loves.

8. PICKING THE BAND

Bands aren't just the main topic of conversation for people with beards and overly-tight T-shirts, they're also the round bit of an engagement ring. And there's a surprising amount to think about.

There's a whole range of metals to choose from – yellow gold, white gold and platinum are among the most popular. Each has its own attributes, and a different price tag. Some of the differences are pronounced, while others would be missed by the untrained eye.

You should consider the advantages and disadvantages of each before making your purchase. Gold is extremely shiny and easy to polish up if it dulls, but it's a soft metal, which means it will wear over time. By contrast, platinum is durable and will last a long time, but it dulls more quickly than gold and doesn't buff up to its original lustre.

This chapter will help you to decide things like whether it's worth spending on platinum over white gold and 18 karat gold over 9 karat.

Gold

Prized by the ancient Egyptians, Aztecs, Romans and the dragon in Shrek, gold's rarity and sparkle means it has always been valued above its usefulness as a metal.

The earliest gold coins date back to 2,700BC,[9] while the oldest jewellery is from way back around 4,200BC.[10]

But despite its long history and extensive mining since the 19th century, if you add up all the gold that's ever been mined in the whole history of the world you get just 174,000 tonnes.[11] That's the same as the amount of trash that the USA produces in just 40 minutes.[12] Was that stat impressive? I'm not sure, but the bottom line is that although there seems to be a lot of it, it's actually quite rare. And we should all probably recycle more.

Gold is a soft metal, so is rarely found in pure form, other than gold ingots. If you took one of the bricks from Fort Knox and pressed your thumbnail into it, you would leave a mark, so for this reason, gold is combined with other metals to add strength. The proportion of gold in the resulting alloy gives the karat rating:

- 9 karat = 9/24 = 37.5% pure gold

- 14 karat = 14/24 = 58.3% pure gold

- 18 karat = 18/24 = 75% pure gold

- 24 karat = 24/24 = 100% gold

Most jewellery grade gold is either classified as 9 karat or 18 karat gold.

Nine karat is springier and more difficult to bend out than 18 karat, so a ring with a fine band is less likely to bend out of shape if it's 9 karat rather than 18. However, if a ring is sturdily constructed, then neither will bend out of shape.

A difference that is obvious to the naked eye is the difference in colour between the two. Eighteen karat gold has a richer golden colour than 9 karat, and will retain this colour and lustre better as it ages.

With a much higher percentage of gold in 18 karat, you might expect it to be considerably more expensive than 9 karat, and it is nearly twice as pricey on a per-gram basis. But with the small amounts of gold used in rings, the difference in price is not too great in the overall cost of an engagement ring.

If you're going for gold and you can stretch to it, 18 karat is the one to go for, as long as the ring is not lightweight. It offers a richer colour and it will age better.

White gold

White gold starts life as yellow gold but is then plated with rhodium, which has many of the same properties as platinum including the white colour.[13] The coating is between 8-10 atoms thick, and although it is durable, it may eventually wear away, meaning the ring will return to the colour of the gold underneath.

While 9 karat and 18 karat white gold have a similar finish when new, as the coating rubs off the difference between them will be more obvious.

Rose gold

Rose gold is gold tinted with a copper alloy to give it a pink hue. The actual colour depends on the amount of copper in the alloy - the higher the percentage, the darker the hue. So, compared to an 18 karat gold ring, a 9 karat rose gold ring will have a lower proportion of gold and higher proportion of copper in the alloy, giving it deeper pink tones.

Although it can look lovely on women, if you plan to match your wedding ring to hers, you should avoid rose gold unless you are comfortable wearing such a feminine colour.

Platinum

Platinum is the rarest metal on the list – less than 10% of the volume of gold is mined each year. It's found mainly in South Africa and a large proportion of what's produced is for industrial use – mainly in car catalytic convertors and lab equipment. Most jewellery-grade platinum is 95% pure – the remaining 5% is usually copper or titanium.

As mentioned earlier, platinum is extremely durable and the reason for this is because of its density. Although it will still scratch (all metals do), when it does there will be little metal lost.

Another benefit is that it's naturally hypoallergenic, so it won't irritate sensitive skin.

The negatives of platinum are the high price – it's usually about twice as expensive as an equivalent gold band – and it's more difficult to polish up to a brilliant lustre once it has lost its initial sheen.

One thing to consider is that while men often like to buy things they know will last, for women the looks may be more important.

Silver

Silver isn't often used for engagement rings because it's soft and tarnishes easily – even washing hands frequently can dull it and it takes a lot of polishing to get it back up to shininess. While it is less expensive than gold or platinum, it's not recommended for a ring that is going to be worn every day.

Palladium

Palladium is similar to platinum, but less rare. Its use in

jewellery is quite new and it's sold either on its own or as an alloy in white gold. It's flexible, resists tarnishing well and is hypoallergenic.

Its lower density than platinum means it's less expensive, but although it is a similar silver-white in colour, it is darker and greyer than platinum, which affects its bling factor.

Titanium

Titanium is seldom used in engagement rings, but is worth considering for a man's wedding ring. It's sturdy, has a cool matt grey finish, or can be polished black. It's durable, corrosion-resistant and made up a good portion of the Terminator 800's skeleton. All plus points, obviously. As titanium is more plentiful than the other metals mentioned, it's also less expensive.

Matching the bands

There are two parts to matching an engagement ring that need to be considered:

1. Matching your wife's wedding ring to her engagement ring

2. Matching your own wedding ring (if you choose to wear one)

With your wife-to-be's wedding and engagement rings, you should make sure they look like they were designed to be worn together. They should complement each other in both colour and shape.

The easiest way is to choose the same metal for both rings.

As well as the look of the rings together, the hardness of

the metals needs to be taken into account. As explained earlier, platinum is much harder than white gold, so when they rub together the gold will come off worse. The rhodium layer will be the first to be worn away. That wouldn't be the end of the ring – you could get it re-plated, but it would be an additional hassle and expense.

I'd recommend keeping the same material for the engagement and wedding rings – they'll wear well together as they age.

The second thing is to match your ring with hers, if you choose to wear one.

In days of yore, men's and women's wedding rings would be bought together, as a set. The man's would be chunkier, but the design would be the same. This fell out of fashion as women's rings became ornate. While they used to be just a plain band, now they often incorporate a row of diamonds. Unless you're Snoop Dogg, you're probably going to struggle to pull this off.

A common tradition now is for the two rings to match in colour as best they can. So, the rule of thumb would be to choose your wife's wedding ring first and then one for yourself that will complement it, rather than being an exact match.

9. SIZING

Something that seems simple but is actually quite confusing is the size of the ring. Getting the size wrong isn't the biggest deal – it can be inexpensively changed – but could make the engagement process less perfect than it should be.

When you drop to one knee, the light shines down from above, the choir breaks into song etc. etc., you want to make sure that you can deftly slide the ring onto her dainty hand with Clooney-like smoothness. You don't want to ham-fistedly jam it on there, crushing a couple of finger-joints in the process.

How ring sizes work

There are a few different measurement standards, but they all basically gauge the inside circumference of the band. The international standard measures in millimetres; the US & Canada have a scale that goes up in roughly 1/10 of an inch; the rest of the English-speaking world uses an alphabetical system; some of Europe sticks to the international standard, while other parts take the circumference in millimetres and minus 40 to give a rating; and India, Japan and China use a totally different system which doesn't seem to reference either the diameter or circumference. Glad that's all clear then.

I've included a table to show all of the different sizing scales and how they relate to each other at the appendix at the back of the book. It's useful to see how the scales compare and also in case you want to buy a ring from another country.

Finding the right size for her

A well-known piece of advice for finding the correct engagement ring size is to wrap a piece of string around your girlfriend's ring finger while she sleeps and then measure that. But unless she sleeps like a hibernating grizzly bear, I'd avoid this. You'll risk waking her up and ruining any element of surprise.

The very easiest way to find out is if she wears a ring on the same finger of her opposite hand. 'Borrow' the ring and either take it to any jeweller who will be able to measure its inside circumference and tell you the size you need for your engagement ring. Or, if borrowing the ring is too risky, you can use my ring measurer.

I've created a printable tool which includes all of the standard ring sizes, so you can measure any existing ring and find the correct size. If she doesn't wear a ring on her fourth finger, you can estimate from the size of a ring from either the middle finger or index finger by dividing the circumference of either by 1.1 to get her ring finger size.

If you've decided to involved your girlfriend in the ring hunt, I've also included a printable finger measurer which you can use to measure her finger and make sure you get it spot on.

Either of these two options will take the guess work out of getting the right size. Download the tool from www.ring-measurer.com.

If all else fails

If she doesn't wear any rings, or if you live far away from her, or if none of these methods will work for any other reason, you can estimate from average ring sizes.

Based on a 5'4", 140lbs girl the average ring size is:

Inside Diameter		Inside Circumference		Sizes			
(in)	(mm)	(in)	(mm)	US & Canada	UK & ANZ	BRIC	EU
0.65	16.51	2.04	51.9	6	L.1/2	11	11.75

If she's more slender or petite than the average girl, her ring size will be smaller – probably in the 4 1/2 to 5 1/2 (US) range. If she's taller or larger then she's more likely to be 6 1/2 to 7 1/2 (US). You can use the table to convert to your local measurement.[14]

Resizing

Lastly, remember that almost all rings can be easily resized, but it's easier to size down than up. The exceptions to this are rings which have stones all the way around the band - these can't be resized.

Do your best to get the size right, but if in doubt err on the size of caution and go larger. That way you'll be able to get it on her finger when you pop the question and be able to organise a quick resize after she says yes.

10. DIAMONDS

There is a lot of information out there about diamonds and I've tried to distil it down to only what you need to know. But, despite me wielding my editor's pen like Ron Jeremy does his little fella, there's still an awful lot to get through. However, by the end of the chapter you'll be well versed in diamonds and know what's really important.

I'll kick this section off with a quick geology lesson and a couple of facts which I think are pretty incredible.

Diamonds are formed around 100 miles under the Earth's surface through immense pressure and heat. Just how hot it gets down there is up for debate, but it's estimated to be around 5,400 Fahrenheit. So far, so geography lesson, right? However, what I find amazing is that all the diamonds that we are currently mining and finding were formed between 1 billion and 3 billion years ago, which is 25%-75% of the age of the Earth. So, that rock that you're currently looking at in a jeweller's window could have been formed 3 billion years ago.

To put that in perspective, men arrived on earth just 100,000 years ago, dinosaurs died out 65 million years ago and the only life on the planet 3 billion years ago were single-celled organisms that had just arrived on a meteorite from outer space. Amazing huh?

The Four Cs

The four Cs are the characteristics that define a stone's quality and therefore determine how much it's worth. They are:

- Cut
- Carat
- Colour
- Clarity

I'll talk you through each one – giving you the lowdown on what they are but also telling you how much each actually matters. I'll also throw in one extra – certification, a no-brainer that you need to ensure that you tick off.

The relative importance of each C is up to you and when choosing a diamond you'll need to balance them to make it work within your budget.

Cut

Technically, cut is the symmetry, proportioning and polish of a diamond, rather than the shape. But for this section I'll mix cut and the shape because the two terms are sometimes used interchangeably and they're closely related.

Cut is the factor that most impacts the amount of light which is refracted and reflected back to you and therefore the amount that a diamond sparkles. A well cut diamond will be noticeably sparklier than a poorly cut stone, so it's a characteristic that's definitly worth investing in.

As cut is the only characteristic not related to the way the diamond was formed (3 billion years ago!), it's the area most open to errors and bad practices. If a diamond is cut incorrectly it can compromise the sparkle and even a diamond that scores highly on other factors will lose its brilliance and most of its value.

I'll talk you through each of the 10 most recognised shapes with a minimum recommended cut spec for each, from a jeweller with 10 years' experience.

Round Brilliant

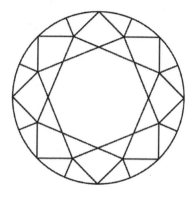

The round cut, or 'brilliant cut' is the classic diamond shape and the most popular. The agreed shape has 58 faces and was first developed by a French mathematician who calculated the angles to reflect the largest amount of light, giving the greatest sparkle.

The top cut is known as 'excellent' and is the one that reflects the most light entering the diamond back to your eyes.[15]

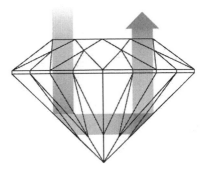

If the diamond is cut too shallow, the majority of the light will pass straight and won't bounce back, making it appear opaque and 'glassy':

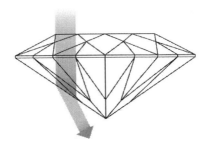

If the stone is cut too deep the light will reflect back at the wrong angle, making it appear smaller from the top and with a black centre, known as a 'nailhead'

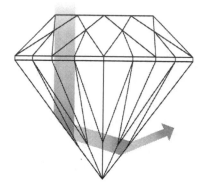

As with most things in life, the higher quality something is, the rarer and more expensive it is.

Here's how the brilliant cut diamond scale works:

- Excellent cut: Restricted to the top 3% of diamond quality. They reflect nearly all light to give the brightest sparkle.

- Very good cut: The top 15% of diamond quality. While not as high quality as the 'excellent', they reflect nearly as much light, at a lower price.

- Good cut: Top 25%. Reflects most light and is significantly less expensive than 'very good'.

- Fair cut: Top 35%. Still decent quality, but noticeably less brilliant.

- Poor cut: All of the rest!

To make things nicely complicated, some authorities

include 'Ideal' above 'excellent', and then to really keep it interesting some manufacturers include their own 'signature cut' grading level above excellent as well.

My recommendation would be to go with 'excellent' if you can afford it, or very good as a minimum. For a round brilliant diamond, my recommended spec is:

- Cut: Very Good+

- Colour: H+

- Clarity: SI1+

Don't worry – we'll get to colour and clarity shortly, and the rest of the recommendation will make much more sense!

Princess

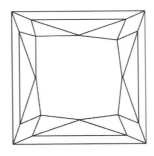

The princess cut is the second most popular shape. It's square from the top, tapering to a point at the bottom, like an upside down pyramid.

A princess cut with the same width as a round brilliant will weigh more due to the extra material on the corners. Because it retains more of the original rough diamond (around 80%), princess diamonds are cheaper than brilliant cuts (which result in more wastage of the rough as they only retain about 50% of the original rock).

When cut correctly, a princess cut will sparkle just as brightly as an ideal cut brilliant diamond. But, unlike a brilliant cut, there's no official cut scale. However, many jewellers do still include cut grading in their specs for Princess shaped stones and all of the other stones in this chapter. A recommendation for achieving a good sparkle is:

- Cut: Very Good+
- Colour: G+
- Clarity: SI1+

Emerald shape

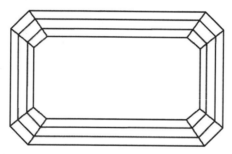

The emerald cut is rectangular and most closely resembles the natural diamond shape. As it has fewer facets and is not optimised to reflect light back, emerald cut diamonds aren't as brilliant as round or princess cuts, but some people consider it a little classier. It's timeless and elegant, rather than bold and flashy. More Keira Knightly than Kim Kardashian.

One thing to note is that because it has a large 'table' (the bit on top), flaws, imperfections and darker colours can be easier to see, so you may need a diamond with a higher clarity and colour grade than a brilliant or a princess cut.

However, as they're not as popular as the round brilliant or the princess cut, emerald cut diamonds are less expensive than both, so if you go for this style, you can put your budget into higher quality in other areas.

Recommended minimum specs for the emerald are:

- Cut: Very Good
- Colour: G+
- Clarity: VS2+

Radiant

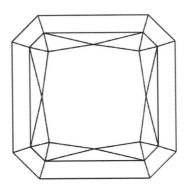

The radiant is the emerald cut's younger, flashier sister. The Pippa Middleton to the emerald cut's Princess Kate. Looking pretty similar, the radiant has more facets and the increase has a similar effect to the round brilliant cut – it reflects a large amount of light and sparkles brightly.

Recommended minimum specs are:

- Cut: Very Good
- Color: H+
- Clarity: SI1+

Asscher

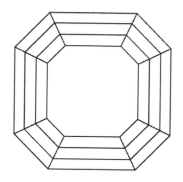

The Asscher diamond is another old cut which has recently become more popular as Hollywood stars like Angelina Jolie have chosen it. It's a stepped cut and is sometimes called the 'square emerald cut' because of the similarities. It's a flashy cut but you can get away with a lower clarity rating because the steps obscure some of the light coming through.

Recommended minimum specs are:

- Cut: Good
- Color: G+
- Clarity: VS2+

Pear

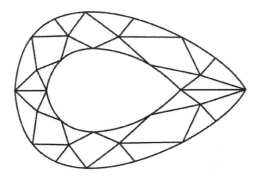

The pear is a modified brilliant shape, so has many facets to reflect the light. It's usually worn with the point facing forwards, which gives a slimming effect.

A couple of things to watch out for are uneven shoulders, when the bottom rounded edge isn't symmetrical, and the 'bow tie effect', which is a dark section in the shape of a bow tie on the top. The bow tie effect is easy to spot – if it has it, you'll know it.[16]

Minimum recommended specs:

- Cut: Good
- Color: G
- Clarity: SI2
- Length/Width Ratio: 1.45:1 - 1.70:1

Oval

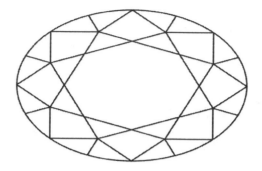

Again, the oval diamond shares many of the assets of the round brilliant cut, but is often chosen by people who want a less common cut. It can also be a good way to get a ring that appears larger than a round brilliant, at the same price.

Minimum recommended specs:

- Cut: Very Good
- Color: G
- Clarity: SI2
- Length/Width Ratio: 1.33:1 - 1.66:1

Heart

One for the romantics, but possibly bordering on a tad cheesy, the heart cut is rare due to the level of wastage of diamond needed to achieve it.

Recommended specs:

- Cut: Good
- Colour : G
- Clarity: SI2

Marquise

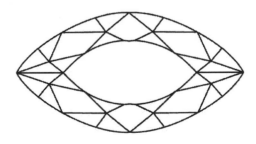

According to legend, the first marquise diamond was commissioned in 18th century Paris by the philandering

King Louis XV to emulate the smile of his mistress. Although it's not a commonly found cut, the marquise can have a slimming effect on fingers, so if you think that this might be beneficial for you other half then it could be worth considering.

Minimum specs:

- Cut: Good
- Color: G
- Clarity: SI2

Cushion

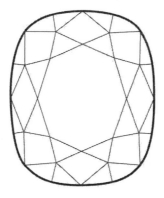

Also know as a 'pillow cut', the cushion has been around for more than a century. With a larger visible area than some of the other cuts, I'd recommended going slightly higher with clarity, as imperfections may be more noticeable.

Minimum specs:

- Cut: Very Good+
- Color: G+
- Clarity: VS2

Which cut to go for?

The real answer is whichever you like the most. Cuts go in and out of fashion, and while round brilliants are the most popular now and look likely to retain their value the best, as you're not buying it as an investment, this shouldn't matter.

If you're still not sure, the table overleaf has character traits related to different cuts. Saul Spero spent 25 years interviewing over 50,000 women to find out if there was any relationship between favourite diamond shape and personality and came out with these results:[17]

Shape	Personality Trait
Round	Family-centered, dependable, unaggressive.
Oval	Individual, creative, well-organised, willing to take chances.
Heart	Sentimental, feminine, sensitive, trusting.
Rectangle /Square	Disciplined, conservative, efficient, honest.
Pear	Conforming, considerate, adaptable.
Marquise	Extroverted, aggressive, innovative, career-centered.

I'd probably recommend taking these findings with a hefty pinch of salt, but if you want a gentle nudge in one direction, they could be useful.

Detailed cut info

For even more detail on cuts, check out www.diamondcut.gia.edu to find the Gemological Association of America's rules for determining cut grade.

Colour

The second of the four Cs. The rarest and the most valuable colour for a diamond is 'white', or colourless, while more common diamonds tend to be darker and more yellow. The closer to white a diamond is, the more light it lets pass through, which means it sparkles more brilliantly. As you've guessed by now, the sparklier a diamond, the spendier it is.

Diamonds are ranked on a scale, from D to Z. I'm not sure what happened to A, B and C, but we've got to work with what we're given here.

As this is a continuous scale, the difference between each increment can be very small.

While an F diamond is classified as 'colourless' and a G is only 'near colourless', it's actually very difficult to see any difference between them with the naked eye, especially if they are not placed directly next to each other. The most common level for engagement rings is G or H - just between 'colourless' and 'near colourless'.

While the 'best' diamond is one that is completely colourless, exceptions are made if a diamond has a very strong and distinct colour. The most expensive diamond in the world was a rose tinted 'fancy' diamond which sold for $83 million in November 2013.[18]

Watch out:

A big factor when deciding on colour is which setting you are going with. With white gold or platinum, you should go as colourless as possible – in the D-G range, otherwise the coloured stone will look more yellow when compared with the brilliant white colour of the setting. If you're going with a gold setting then it's a bit more forgiving; you can go down to J before the stone starts to appear noticeably yellow.

Clarity

The third C, clarity, is a measure of the number of flaws visible through a jeweller's magnifying eyeglass (known as a loupe), although they are usually invisible to the naked eye. The 'inclusions' are tiny imperfections that arose naturally when the diamond was being formed and show up as white pinpoints, feather-like shapes or cloudy areas in the stone. Some people will tell you they are 'nature's fingerprint' and that their presence makes a diamond unique, but these are the same people who probably don't wash their hands after going to the bathroom.

The most common system for grading diamonds is the Gemological Institute of America's scale, overleaf. Although I know that there are a few rows on this table, and tables are boring, it's worth paying attention to the third column which explains how the diamonds are graded.

Acronym	Description	Traits
FL	Flawless	Extremely rare, with only a few hundred found each year
IF	Internally Flawless	Only external flaws are present, which can be removed by further polishing the stone
VVS1	Very Very Slightly Included 1	Only an expert can detect flaws with a 10X microscope. If an expert can only detect flaws when viewing the bottom of the stone, then it is a VVS1
VVS2	Very Very Slightly Included 2	Only an expert can detect flaws with a 10X microscope. If an expert can see a flaw from the top of the diamond, it is a VVS2
VS1 - VS3	Very Slightly Included	A layman can see flaws with a 10X microscope, but it takes a long time (more than about 10 seconds)
SI1 - SI2	Slightly Included	A layman can more easily see flaws with a 10X microscope
I1 - I3	Imperfect	You can see flaws with the naked eye. I'd recommend avoiding I1-I3 diamonds.

So, while flawless diamonds have no inclusions at all, it's only when you get down to I1 - the bottom row of the table - that flaws are actually visible to the naked eye.

Slightly Included stones should be eye-clean, with no flaws visible. However, on occasion the graders may get a bit enthusiastic with their reports and a SI2 may not be eye-clean when examined closely. I'd therefore recommend going with SI2 as a minimum for quality, and as a recommendation for the best value.

Unless you think that your fiancée is planning on examining the ring under a microscope, I'd say that it's probably not worth incurring the extra cost of going for a diamond that scores highly on the clarity scale if it's going to look exactly the same to her.

Watch out:
Something to avoid are 'clarity enhanced' diamonds, where stones have fractures filled or are treated with lasers or radiation to dissolve internal flaws. Although they can end up looking nearly flawless as a result, enhanced diamonds are worth less and are less durable than an untreated diamond.

Clarity enhanced diamonds are difficult to detect so ask your jeweller to confirm the diamond is not clarity enhanced and double check this is supported by the certification.

Carat
The fourth and last of the official four Cs, carat is the weight, and therefore the size, of a diamond. One carat is 0.2 grams (or 0.007 ounces for those in the USA and Bangladesh, the only two countries still stubbornly

sticking to the Imperial system). Each carat is divided into 100 smaller units, called points – basically the percentage of a carat.

Confusingly, the measurement of purity for gold is the similarly named 'karat', with a K. However, the two scales are unrelated.

How big should you go? Carat is the factor that most affects the price of a ring, so it depends how much you are willing to spend. Going bigger can make a ring more impressive, but can also result in an impressively big price. Large good quality diamonds are rare so the relationship between size and cost isn't linear - a two carat diamond will cost much, much more than twice the price of a one carat rock.

Theknot.com has conducted a survey which provides some useful benchmarks:

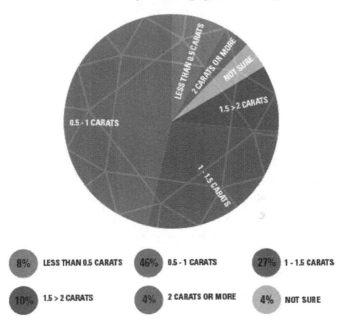

8% LESS THAN 0.5 CARATS	46% 0.5 - 1 CARATS	27% 1 - 1.5 CARATS
10% 1.5 > 2 CARATS	4% 2 CARATS OR MORE	4% NOT SURE

The most common size is 1/2-1 carat and unless your girlfriend has the bratwurst fingers of an East German shot putter, anywhere around 0.7pts will look fine.

Ultimately, the size you go for is up to you, but by following the advice in this chapter when it comes to colour and clarity, you can increase the size of the carat you can afford.

Size isn't everything – if you go for the biggest diamond at the lowest price, you'll compromise on the other Cs to such an extent that the stone will look inferior when compared with other diamonds.

Certification

Not an official 'C', not very exciting, but definitely very

important, you need to ensure that any diamond that you're looking at is a 'cert stone', which means that it has been assessed, graded and coded with a laser by an independent lab.

The lab to trust and to look for certification from is the non-profit Gemological Institute of America (GIA). It's the most internationally recognised and genreally seen as the most impartial of all of the gem labs.

Others are part of trade bodies that contain jewellery retailers, or are 'for profit'. While the GIA is very consistent with its gradings, the others have a reputation for being overly. What the GIA say is merely a diamond with a 'good' cut, maybe be graded 'excellent' by another lab, with an excellently large price to match.

Each certificate has a unique report number and detailed information about the stone, covering the four Cs, the height, depth and other info.

As well as providing assurance that the stone that you're buying is the quality that you are paying for, a certificate also proves what you're buying is not a substitute. Substitutes can either be natural materials like zircon, white sapphire, topaz or quartz, or 'synthetic' like cubic zirconia and moissanite. These stones are legitimately sold as cheap alternatives and costume jewellery, and can be convincing. Although it's rare that anyone would try to pass them off as a diamond, certification will give you peace of mind.

I interviewed a gemologist who cuts and polishes not just high value gemstones, but also synthetic substitutes like cubic zirconia. He told me that he could buy a piece of cubic zirconia and cut a 3 carat brilliant-cut stone that would be nearly indistinguishable from a real diamond by anyone other than a gemologist. It would cost him just $5 for the rough stone plus a little bit of his time, as opposed to roughly $40,000 for the real thing.

I was flabbergasted by this, and started to question whether it was worth spending on a real diamond. If no one can tell the difference, what's the point?

Well, although when they were both brand new they would be nearly indistinguishable, as time goes on a ring that's worn every day gets knocked and a soft stone like a cubic zirconia can get easily damaged. The beauty of a diamond is that it is so hard and won't chip no matter what you throw at it. A zirconia, however, will chip easily and very quickly won't be looking like the real deal anymore.

Also, the more I thought about it, the more I realised it wasn't the physical properties of the diamond that I was buying, it was what the diamond meant. It's a symbol of love, commitment and sacrifice that I was prepared to make for my wife-to-be.

I also realised she would kick my arse if she ever found out I'd tried to palm her off with a fake.

One last thing that certification will show is whether a stone has been artificially treated and clarity enhanced. Although it's legal to treat diamonds, they're worth less than untreated diamonds so all treatments must be listed on the certification.

To sum it all up

When buying a diamond engagement ring, it really is about finding a balance of the 4 Cs that fits into your budget and gives you the result that you are looking for.

Remember what was listed as important for girls in chapter 4 and think about your own other half and what will be important for her.

The one recommendation that I would definitely make is to ensure that you don't scrimp on the 'cut', as this will have the biggest impact on how much your ring sparkles.

I go into a few more tips to make sure you get the most bling for your buck in Chapter 14: Making Your Money Go Further.

11. BLOOD DIAMONDS

'Blood diamonds', or 'conflict diamonds' mainly refer to diamonds from West Africa and Angola, where slave labour was used to illegally mine and export them, with the proceeds used to fund civil wars. The issue came into public consciousness when it was linked to the horrific war crimes in those regions in the late '90s and was cemented by Leonardo DiCaprio and his shocking Suth Efricken accent in the film Blood Diamond.

Thankfully the majority of the conflicts in Africa that were funded by conflict diamonds have ended, although there are still some conflict diamond issues in The Ivory Coast. There is now a process which aims to make sure diamonds are obtained legally and are not funding any wars.

The Kimberley Process, named after the town in South Africa where the agreement was signed,[19] says that every time a diamond changes hands from the mine to the retailer, the seller must declare it was mined using UN-approved methods or that they bought it from someone who gave this assurance.

It works pretty well, and since 2002 it's been illegal to import diamonds without Kimberly Certification into the

US, Canada, Europe, Australia and most of the rest of the world. So, if you're buying a diamond from a legit source in any of these countries, you shouldn't have too much to worry about.

If you want to make sure you avoid conflict diamonds, you have a few options:

- Buy a diamond that was mined in Canada or Australia – they both have their own certification schemes that prove the diamond was mined and processed in their own countries. You will, however, pay a large premium for this peace of mind

- Buy a vintage diamond that was mined before the issues in Africa started

- Buy another gemstone, instead of a diamond

However, to boycott diamonds from Africa entirely would harm those the Kimberley process helps. It has brought huge volumes of diamonds onto the legal market that would not otherwise have made it there. In Sierra Leone, legal exports have increased 100-fold since the end of the war in 2002, bringing benefits to 10% of the population who depend on the diamond industry.[21]

By asking to see a copy of a retailer's policy on conflict diamonds and finding out how they can be sure the stones comply with the Kimberley Process, you can buy with a clear conscience.

12. DOES IT NEED TO BE A DIAMOND?

I talked about how diamonds came to be the de facto choice for modern engagement rings in Chapter 2: A Brief History of Engagement Rings, but there are alternative stones. Maybe you've always known you wanted to do something a little unusual for your lady, or maybe she has hinted that she wants something a bit more alternative.

Choosing a different stone can also be a less expensive way to get a fantastic ring, but there are some things to watch out for.

A diamond is forever

De Beers' clever tagline has truth in it. Diamonds scores a perfect 10 on "Moh's scale", which is used to rank the hardness of minerals.[22] The scale is relative and was created by scraping two materials together and seeing which one gets scratched. The harder material goes above the softer one in the scale and by testing all materials against each other, we get the relative hardness of all materials. Diamond stands proud at the top of the table as the hardest naturally-occurring material on Earth, other than Chuck Norris.

This hardness makes it an ideal material for rings that will be worn every day – it's tough enough to survive day-to-day knocks and the occasional drunken tumble from a taxi.

Moh money, Moh problems?

Hardness is a big factor when looking at alternative stones for use in an engagement ring. Luckily, there are some other common precious stones which also score highly on Moh's scale and can make suitable centre stones.

Scoring a 9 is a group of stones called Corundum, which includes sapphires and rubies. Although they are a 9, as the scale is relative one, this just means that they're harder than number 8, topaz, but not as hard as diamond. They're actually four times less hard than diamond, so are much more likely to get scratched and worn down. However, if looked after, they can still stand up well over time.

Other precious stones fare less well. Emeralds score a 7.5 on Moh's scale which means that great care must be taken with them if they are going to be worn every day. The other precious stones which are less commonly used in jewellery are aquamarine, spinel and tourmaline. Again, all of these are between 7 and 8 on the scale and aren't really suitable as the main stone in a ring for daily use. I'll give you a quick run-down on rubies, sapphires and emeralds as these are the most common alternatives to diamonds. I'll also take a very quick look at 'black diamonds', which have become fashionable over the last few years.

Rubies

Rubies and sapphires are technically the same stone – corundum. All red corundums are rubies, and all other colours are sapphires. High quality rubies are actually much rarer than diamonds and their supply has never needed to be artificially restricted like diamonds' has because they're already scarce. As a result, rubies are the most expensive gemstone by carat, other than very rare colours of diamond.

Like all gemstones, rubies are judged on the 4 Cs, but the relative importance of each of the Cs is very different to with diamonds. I'll look at each in order of importance.

Colour

With rubies, the intensity of the red is the main factor that affects desirability and value. A good ruby is an intense, rich crimson, without being too light or dark. Think Manchester United's home shirt. As you get lighter or darker, the value decreases. In fact, lighter stones are sometimes called 'pink sapphires' and the line between the two is unclear. There's an old jeweller's joke: "Whether it's a ruby or a pink sapphire depends on whether you're the buyer or the seller."[23]

Maybe not ROFL-worthy, but it's worth bearing in mind that with all precious gems, some jewellers aren't above trying to pull the wool over buyers' eyes.

To properly gauge the colour of a ruby, it's best to look in daylight, rather than the harsh lights of shops. Fluorescent tubes have no output in the red end of the spectrum, which can make rubies look dull and grey.

Clarity

All rubies will have some inclusions and the value of the

stone depends hugely on how visible these are. The 'flaws' are caused by other minerals that were present when the ruby was originally formed.

In fact, if someone is offering you a 'flawless ruby', then it's almost definitely fake and you should turn around and head on out of there.

However, although flaws are part and parcel of buying a ruby, not all are equal and you need to know what to look out for.

The most severe flaws, and something that you should avoid, are cracks along the surface, which can seriously impact the stone's strength and mean that it could break along the crack. Avoid.

The other type are internal inclusions, and the main thing to watch out for is that they aren't too obvious and that they don't make the colour of the ruby inconsistent or affect the transparency of the stone.

Rubies should be semi-transparent, which means that you should be able to see through them, but you can't expect them to be totally see through like glass.

The test that is often used is to place a newspaper underneath it. You should be able to read the newspaper through it, just. So, if you're looking at a ruby in a jeweller, place some reading material underneath it and see if you can make out the text as you look through it.

Star rubies

One type of 'flaw' that is actually readily accepted is when the inclusions form a star shape, as seen overleaf.

One thing to watch out for with star rubies is that they're liable to have a large number of surface cracks which can weaken the stone and make it less durable.

Treatment

Although inclusions are accepted with rubies, nearly all will have been treated to improve their colour and dissolve some of the imperfections. There are three ways this happens:

- Heat treatment, where the stone is heated nearly to melting point to dissolve the imperfections . This is viewed as a continuation of the heating process that created the stone in the first place and is an accepted practice.

- Diffusion of chromium into the surface of the ruby, which changes a stone's colour and makes it more red. This only affects the first 1/2 a millimetre of the stone, so if it is damaged, the original colour will show through. Stones that have had diffusion treatment are worth significantly less than untreated stones.

- Irradiation involves exposing a ruby to beryllium, which makes it more red. This effect wears off quickly in sunlight, so should definitely be avoided.

When buying, always ensure that the treatments are marked on the certificate that you are given with the stone. Non-treated stones are available, but you'll pay for the privilege. If you are buying an untreated ruby, make sure you organise a third party assessment to make sure you're getting what you pay for.

Cut

While cut is probably the most important factor when choosing a diamond, with rubies it takes a backseat behind colour and clarity. There are some cuts which are more common than others, but ultimately it should just be about finding a shape that you like.

The most common cuts for rubies are ovals or cushions, which maximise the visible area of the top of the stone. Unlike diamonds, the sparkle factor isn't such a big deal, so although there are some round stones out there, it's not as popular as with diamonds.

There's also a cut that isn't used for diamonds – the domed cabochon cut, below. This is often used for star stones to highlight the star itself.

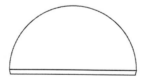

Compared to more modern and more intricate cuts, it's pretty simple, so was easily achieved with the tools that they had available at the time. However, because less workmanship is involved in their production, a cabochon cut ruby is usually worth less than one with a more complicated shape.[24]

One thing to watch out for with the cabochon cut is that there may be a large amount of stone hidden below the setting, which means you're paying for something you can't see.[25]

Carat

The size of a ruby us either measured in mm or in carats, with a diameter in mm often used for stones smaller than 0.5 carats, and the carat scale used above that.

One thing to note is that rubies are dense and heavy compared to other gemstones, which means that a ruby that weighs 1 carat will be smaller than a diamond that weighs the same amount.

When you're comparing different rubies, make sure that you ask the jeweller what the 'price per carat' is for each stone. This will allow you to see how the more important factors, like colour, are affecting the price without the difference in size getting thrown into the mix and confusing you.

Certification

As always, the fifth C is certification. When buying a ruby, make sure that it is accompanied by a certificate from the GIA, AGL or other reputable gem lab - this is especially important to ensure that any treatments that have been applied to the stone are completely detailed.

Don't rely on what the jeweller tells you about the size, clarity or treatments applied to the stone – make sure that you have it in writing from an independent source to ensure that you aren't getting hoodwinked.

Sapphires

Sapphires are the blue form of corundum and, as I mentioned earlier, they're the same stone as rubies. However, they're more popular than rubies because they're more common, which means that they are less expensive.

That's not to say they're cheap though! A top quality sapphire can still be more expensive than an equivalently sized diamond.

Although you might usually think of sapphires as blue, they actually come in a whole heap of colours, including yellow, green and purple. Different colours are valued differently, and top quality pink or Padparadscha sapphires can be more expensive than a top quality blue one.

Colour

As with rubies, colour is the most important factor that determines quality and value.[26] I'll talk you through each of the colours that sapphires come in:

Blue sapphires:

With blues, the colour can range from light all the way to a deep black/blue, but mid-coloured blues are the most desirable and therefore the most expensive. That's not to say that they're the best – if you find a light or dark blue sapphire that you love for the right price then go for it.

The other sapphire colours, in order of desirability are:

Padparadscha sapphires:

An unusual salmony/orange color, padparadscha is very rare and the most expensive colour.

Pink sapphires:

Pink sapphires can sometimes be called rubies, but their colour can run anywhere from light pink to a very dark pink known as "hot pink".

Purple sapphires:

Squarely in the middle of the pack in terms of desirability and price, they have a wide colour range and can look fantastic.

Yellow sapphires:

Usually reasonably priced as they're found in huge formations. They can look similar to a canary yellow diamond for a fraction of the price.

Green sapphires:

The least popular of all sapphires and priced accordingly.

Clarity

Again, as they're technically the same stone as rubies, flaws are common and expected, as well as sometimes forming the desirable star shape.

And again, there are two types of inclusions that you should look out for:

1. External: Scratches, nicks or abrasions on the surface of the stone. These are considered minor and shouldn't harm the quality of the stone.

2. Internal: Cracks, chips or cavities within the stone. There are a couple of things to watch out for with internal flaws:

    - That they don't reduce the strength of the stone.

    - That they don't block light from passing

through the stone, or affect the consistency of its colour.

As sapphires are the same as rubies, they often receive the same treatments:

- Heat

- Diffusion

- Irradiation

And again, it's extremely important that any treatment that has been applied is marked on the certification

Cut

Sapphires can be found in any of the major cuts, but currently the most popular shapes are round, cushion and oval. A round cut is a favourite for any stone, but is often more expensive. Trimming all of the corners off a stone to make it into a circle means that a lot of the sapphire hits the cutting room floor, so to end up with a decent sized finished rock, you need a much larger rough stone to begin with.

The cushion and oval cuts minimise the wastage and amount of stone that is lost during the cutting process, which means that they are often used for larger stones.

As with rubies, vintage sapphire rings can sometimes be shaped into the cabochon cut – the basic dome shape.

Emeralds

Although there are other green gemstones out there, emeralds have long been the standard. The Wizard of Oz didn't build his city from green sapphires and if you're looking for a green precious stone for your ring, you shouldn't settle for them either.

While sapphires and rubies are variations of corundum, emeralds are actually a stone called beryl. If the green colour is too yellow or blue, it's downgraded from emerald to plain old beryl and the value drops.

Emerald engagement rings do come with a word of warning - their low score of 7.5 on the Moh's scale of hardness means that they are not all that durable. This is important because an engagement ring is usually worn every day and will inevitably suffer a few knocks, which could result in chips or even a completely broken stone.

So, you'll need to have a think about your other half – if she is the very picture of feminine grace (I'm sure she is!), then you might be able to get away with it. However, if she is likely to suffer the odd drunken tumble out of a taxi then I'd recommend going with a stone other than an emerald. Rubies and sapphires both score 9 on Moh's scale and are considerably more resilient than an emerald.

Colour

As with rubies and sapphires, colour is the biggest factor affecting price. The most sought-after emeralds are bluish green to pure green, with vivid colours that are spread across the stone and aren't too dark. However, colour is subjective and I'd recommend examining the emerald that you're looking at to see what you personally like.

An experienced jeweller can actually manipulate the final colour of an emerald by changing the stone's proportions. A deeper cut can darken a paler stone as less light is allowed through, while a dark stone can be lightened by making the cut shallower with a larger top 'table' to allow more light to enter.

Clarity

Emeralds that have no inclusions visible to the naked eye

are rare, so it's generally accepted that all emeralds will have some visible imperfections. However, as with rubies and sapphires the value will drop if the inclusions affect transparency – you should still be able to see through it.

There's one main treatment that is applied to emeralds and that's 'oiling'. This involves the application of natural cedar oil to an emerald, which is then heated. The oil fills some of the crack on the surface of the stone, improving its durability. Cedar oil treatment is widely accepted and shouldn't affect the value of a stone too much.

Some jewellers now use other materials to fulfil this same function – green-coloured resin and plastic polymers are common. These are generally not accepted by the industry and should be avoided.

One thing to note about oiling is that it isn't permanent. After a few years the stone may need to be re-oiled, which you will need to hit up an emerald specialist for. Having the ring cleaned in an ultransonic cleaner or wearing it while when doing the dishes or having a shower can speed up the rate that the treatment wears off.[27]

As with rubies and sapphires, all treatments should be included on the certification that you receive with a stone, with the level of treatment being noted as minor, moderate or significant, with less treatment meaning a stone is worth more.

Cut

Because they are quite fragile, emeralds are difficult to cut well. Jewellers try to cut them to minimise the visibility of the flaws, but also need to be careful to not crack the stone along the line of a surface imperfection.

Emeralds come in two main shapes – the emerald cut and

round. While you can find them in any of the other stone cuts that are out there, these are the two that you're most likely to encounter when looking for a ring.

Emerald Cuts:
Emerald cuts can be either square or rectangular when viewed from the top and both have a stepped cut down the side of the stone and the corners trimmed off.

The corners are trimmed to help with the mounting of the stone in the ring and because without a sticky-outy corner, the stone is less likely to get knocked on something and break.

Round Cuts:
Round cuts are a popular shape at the moment, but are likely to be significantly more expensive than a similarly sized emerald-cut stone due to the difficulty of cutting the fragile stone and the high amount of wastage.

Ruby, sapphire & emerald settings

One thing you need to know is that emeralds usually look better when paired with a 'white' metal – ie. platinum or white gold. Yellow gold can make even a high quality emerald appear yellow, which is something that you should be trying to avoid. For rubies and sapphires, the colour of the setting shouldn't affect the colour of the stone.

Another thing you need to look at is how exposed the stone is in the setting. If it sits high above the setting and is unprotected, then it's probably more likely to take a knock and be damaged.

A halo setting can not only make the ring look more

impressive, but also give the stone a bit of protection.

Taking this one stage further is the 'bezel' setting, which uses a protective rim of metal around the edge of the stone to protect it.

Some people think that this impacts the aesthetics of the ring, but if you are really keen on a softer stone but know that your other half is more than a bit of a klutz then it is definitely worth considering.

Buying unmounted

Buying a coloured stone unmounted ie. not as part of a ring, can be a good idea for a couple of reasons:

You'll be able to more clearly check out the colour and clarity. This is important because these factors affect the price of the stone hugely.

You can still propose with just the stone, and can then choose the setting with your other half after she has said yes. Again, you get to keep the element of surprise but by getting her involved in picking out the setting, you will make sure that you get a ring that she loves.

One thing to look out for if you are buying the stone unmounted is to make sure that you use a jeweller who has plenty of experience with mounting that type of stone in a setting - this is especially important with emeralds. It's not uncommon for inexperienced jewelers to apply too much pressure to an emerald and crack it, so aim for someone who has good experience and really knows what they're doing.

Black diamonds

I've included black diamonds with alternatives to diamonds because they're not really diamonds.

Black diamonds have become more popular in the last 10 years because of extensive marketing, but have historically been viewed as poor quality and unsuitable for jewellery because they don't have the sparkliness of white diamonds.

And while some jewellers may tell you that black diamonds are every bit as much diamonds as white ones, they actually aren't.

White diamonds are single crystals of carbon, and it's this singular nature that allows light to come in, bounce around and be reflected back with no obstructions, making them shine and sparkle.

Black diamonds are indeed compacted carbon in the same way as white diamonds are, but instead of being one single crystal of carbon, they're made up of many individual crystals mashed together. These sit in front of each other, and at different angles, which bounces the light in different directions, preventing the light from being reflected back to your eye, absorbing it, and resulting in the black colour.[28]

So, while black diamonds are currently quite popular, it's likely that in the future they will fall out of fashion again and they will lose their current value. They just don't have the characteristics that have given white diamonds, rubies, emeralds and sapphires such longevity.

13. WHERE TO BUY

Fifteen years ago, all rings would have been bought from high street jewellers. Chaps would have toddled off with their wallets bulging with three months' salary and taken their pick from the limited selection available.

Now with the rise of e-commerce there are other routes to market for diamonds and small-scale artisanal jewellers give you more options than ever before.

In this section, I'll look at the pros and cons of each of the five main avenues to help you get the ring you want at a price you're happy to pay.

1. Buying from a jeweller

The most traditional option. You can gauge the quality of the shop from its appearance, you'll be able to compare different stores' wares, you can ask sales staff questions and you should be able to examine any diamond through a loupe, or even a microscope.

If you're in a major city, there are often clusters of jewellers, which makes the comparison even easier. Once you know what you're looking for, you can take the specs to each jeweller and see who has the best match and the best price.

Something to watch out for is that in a jewellery shop you may feel like you're being sold to, rather than being free to buy without pressure from a salesperson. I know that when I was first researching engagement rings I felt under immediate pressure from the sales guy in the first jeweller that I visited. I just wanted to have a quick look and find out some rough prices, but I was immediately shown trays and trays of rings and felt that he was trying to get me to make a decision before I left the store. Fair enough, he was just trying to do his job, but I didn't enjoy the experience. Chapter 15 covers buying from a jeweller and how to negotiate to make sure you get the best deal.

When you're looking for a jeweller, you want one that specialises in diamonds, or the precious stone that you're looking for, rather than a generalist. If they have cabinets of crystal decanters and sell fashion designer-branded watches then it's unlikely that they really know their stuff when it comes to engagement rings.

A few questions to consider when selecting a jeweller:

- Do they offer GIA certification?

- Do they offer a written money-back guarantee? Reputable jewellers should offer a cooling off period after purchase.

- Will they let you examine a diamond under a microscope, rather than just through a jeweller's loupe?

- Do they have a full-spectrum diamond light to let you judge the colour grade?

- Do they offer clarity-enhanced diamonds?

Most respectable diamond specialists don't.[29]

2. Jewellery wholesalers

Wholesalers take a link out of the supply chain, resulting in one less person to take a cut of the ring and therefore usually lower prices. They're where the high street jewellers buy their stones and some won't deal with individual consumers.

If you can find a wholesaler that will deal with you then make sure you know exactly what you want before you walk in. They won't be interested in casual enquiries and won't take the time to talk you through options. However, they will have a huge selection of stones, which could be considerably cheaper than a high street jeweller.

Contact your local jewellery trade association for a list of names and numbers. The potential savings are worth an hour of letting your fingers do the walking.

Wholesalers will usually only sell you a stone, rather than a whole ring – you'll need a jeweller for the setting. If you're going to try this route, I'd recommend getting a quote for a setting before you buy the stone, to allow you to work out your budget for the stone.

3. Custom

There are two main reasons to go with a custom ring.

1. If you have an idea for a ring that you can't find elsewhere

2. If you'd like to copy an expensive or rare ring

The benefits of a custom ring are pretty obvious – you can dial-in the different factors of the stone and style the setting to create exactly what you want. Often the best way is to use a small, independent jewellery designer. They will offer a consultative service and work with you on the design until you are happy.

One disadvantage is that you may not have as much haggle-room as with a jeweller. By its nature, a custom-designed piece isn't sitting in a stock-room waiting to be sold, so you'll have to accept the price given to you. But this doesn't mean you won't get a competitive price that can be equivalent to or even lower than a store. The designer and independent manufacturer will have lower overheads which should be reflected in the price.

4. Second hand

Engagement rings mean so much that going for a second hand ring is often overlooked. People want their ring to be freshly cut and polished and untouched by anyone else's finger.

But there are advantages to buying second hand – namely cost savings. Like a car, a diamond will lose significant value as soon as it's driven off the lot – usually around 25%. Despite this, it's still the same quality of diamond and, after a good clean, should look as good as new.

You may also be able to find a fantastic old design not commonly produced now – possibly an art deco gem from the 1930s. If your girlfriend has an offbeat style, a vintage 'preloved' ring could be perfect.

Some old-fashioned shapes and styles also offer great bargains. Old mine cut, transition cut and old European cut diamonds aren't generally sought after. They're often recut to the round brilliant cut, which results in up to 40% of the diamond being lost as the edges are trimmed off. With these cuts you can get a bigger stone at a smaller price.

With a second hand diamond, always make sure it comes with certification. If not, even if you love it, don't buy it unless the seller is willing to get the stone tested by an accredited laboratory, at their cost.

5. Online retailers

Buying a ring or just a stone online offers you the choice from the biggest range possible. Many sites list entire wholesalers' inventories - literally hundreds of thousands of stones - giving you access to a huge choice that a store could never match. And, as with all e-commerce, prices are often lower than traditional stores.

But, the number one reason for buying online is that certain sites have tools that allow you to dial in the characteristics of the ring to your requirements. You can choose the exact combinations of the 4Cs that you want and their huge inventories mean that they will always have a stone to match your specs.

That's what I did when I bought my ring and it meant that I could play with the different factors of the ring until it was exactly what I was looking for. This was definitely the best route for me as it meant that I could use my new knowledge about what really mattered with diamonds, rather than being limited to choosing from a much smaller selection in a bricks and mortar store.

Taking advantage of these tools is a huge pro tip from me and I think that it really is the key to getting a great ring at a fantastic price. As this worked out so well for me, I want to give everyone the chance to benefit from the same service, so I'm building a list of online stores that offer these customisation tools on my website.

How To Buy An Engagement Ring

I'm only including the stores that offer the best selection, the best service and the best prices. Navigate to www.ring-retailers.com to check out the stores that made the cut.

Some people may not be comfortable with buying online, especially with such a high-value purchase, but the stores that I recommend are all extremely well established with excellent reputations and solid return policies. Hopefully you won't need them, but they're there if you do.

Even if you think you are going to buy from a bricks and mortar store, I'd really recommend that you have a quick look at these retailers to conduct a quick price comparison. The difference will probably surprise you!

One thing to note is that as rings bought online are custom-made to your specifications, you do need to allow time for the jeweller to create the ring - usually around four weeks from order to delivery. If you're getting ready to propose though then it's definitely worth building this into your timeline - the increase in value that you will receive will make the wait worth it.

And a last thing to remember is that if I haven't yet found a recommended retailer in your country and you are going to buy from an online store located overseas, tax and duty may be charged when the ring is imported. Do a little research on importing into your country and ensure that you have included any potential taxes in your budget.

14. MAKING YOUR MONEY GO FURTHER

In Chapter 3 we looked at the importance of setting a budget that works for you and throughout the book I've given some tips on where you can scrimp and where you should splurge. Now I'll tie it all together so you're clear on just how you can get the very best ring that you can for your budget.

Now obviously buying an engagement ring shouldn't be based purely on cost - the ring you choose is a symbol of commitment to the person you're going to spend the rest of your life with. But budget and cost are definitely factor - you want to make sure that you get a fantastic ring and don't want go get ripped off. This chapter will help you get the most value that you can.

We're going to look at each of the variables that you can change in a ring and see how they affect the price you pay, to help you decide where to spend and where to save. Some of the info here only applies to diamonds, while the rest can help you with rubies, sapphires or any other stone.

A quick warning - there are a fair few tables in this chapter. However, each is worth paying attention to as they will all help you to get best ring that you can at a price that is right for you.

Choose your shape carefully

There are 10 common shapes for precious stones and each has a different price attached to them. The price is dependent on a few things: their popularity, how much workmanship is involved in creating them, how difficult it is to cut them well, how much of the rough stone is lost to the cutting-room floor etc.

When I started researching for my ring, I knew that round brilliant cuts were by far the most popular shape for diamonds, so I assumed that they would be the most expensive - Econ101 taught me well. But I had no idea about how the rest of the shapes would measure up, so I conducted a quick experiment.

Using one of my recommended online retailers, I looked at each of the diamond shapes in turn and recorded their price, then compared the prices. Pretty simple, right?

To keep the test fair I chose to look at diamonds on their own, rather than stones mounted in a ring setting, and kept all the other characteristics of the stone (colour, clarity and carat) the same. The only thing that I changed was the diamond shape.

The results actually blew my mind a little bit and I'm really pleased to be able to share this information with you so that you can benefit too.

To clarify the controls, I selected a 1 carat stone, with colour F, ideal cut and VS1 clarity. I chose 1 carat stone because it was a nice round number, so don't be put off if the amounts in the table are more than you were planning on spending. The important thing to note is the relative difference in price between the stone shapes.

The table below shows the price for each shape in dollars and then the difference in both dollars and as a percentage from the most expensive, in descending order.

Shape	Price ($)	Difference ($)	Difference (%)
Round	9,215	0	0
Marquise	6,317	-2,898	-31.4
Princess	6,122	-3,093	-33.6
Pear	6,002	-3,213	-34.9
Oval	5,970	-3,245	-35.3
Radiant	5,948	-3,267	-35.5
Heart	5,774	-3,441	-37.3
Cushion	5,677	-3,538	-38.4
Asscher	5,384	-3,831	-41.6
Emerald	5,221	-3,994	-43.3

As you look down the third and fourth columns, you can see the huge difference in percentage, and in real dollars, that changing the shape of the stone can have.

If you're looking at a 1 carat stone, by choosing any other shape than a round brilliant you will automatically save yourself $3,000 - a huge 30%..

And this can rise to over 40% for some shapes.

This floored me when I first conducted this experiment - I really didn't expect the difference to be as big as it is. If your girlfriend hasn't specifically requested a round brilliant shape and there is another shape that you like then you can save yourself thousands over the majority of guys who plump for the round just because that is what everyone else seems to get.

I've since done it a few more times to verify the findings and the results aren't always exactly the same. The one thing that never changes is that the round brilliant is always the most expensive and the other shapes offer considerable savings, but the exact order of the other stones can change. Have a play and see what sort of results you get.

The money you save by being smart with the shape you choose can be put towards other attributes of the ring.

Or, y'know, a weekend in Vegas..

Don't be a clarity case

As I covered in chapter 10, clarity is the one C of diamonds that you can go far down the scale on and still get a diamond that looks great. In fact, you can go almost all the way to the bottom of the scale and you should still not be able to see any inclusions with the naked eye - a microscope is needed to see them.

To demonstrate how clarity affects price, I headed back to the same online retailer for another experiment. Again, I kept the control variables very similar: round ideal cut, Colour F, 1 carat weight.

The pricing results as I moved down the clarity scale, from most expensive to least expensive are overleaf.

Clarity	Price ($)	Difference ($)	Difference (%)
IF	11,711	0	0
VVS1	10,832	-879	-7.5
VVS2	9,421	-2,290	-19.6
VS1	9,215	-2,496	-21.3
VS2	8,401	-3,310	-28.3
SI1	7,598	-4,113	-35.1
SI2	5,872	-5,839	-49.9
I1	5,677	-6,034	-51.5

As with shape, there's an absolutely huge difference between the top and the bottom ranking - this time over 50%. However, the bottom ranking for clarity is definitely to be avoided – 'I' means 'Imperfect' and stones that have been graded at this level will it have inclusions that are visible to the naked eye.

If you move up the scale to 'Slightly Included 2' and above, have all been certified as being 'eye clean' i.e. although inclusions are present, they should be only visible through a microscope and should appear clean to the naked eye.

For me, the grading to go for is SI1 – Slightly Included 1. Although flaws can be seen when the stone is examined through a 10x microscope, they will still be eye-clean. Going with SI1 rather than SI2 avoids the risk that the certifier was slightly generous with their grading and bumped up an Imperfect 1 to and Slightly Included 2.

A SI1 stone is a whopping 35% cheaper than an

Internally Flawless stone, but unless they are compared under a microscope, no-one would be able to tell the difference between them.

Size isn't everything

How big a stone looks isn't a direct reflection of its carat weight. A large proportion of any set stone is hidden beneath the bezel of the ring setting, so an increase in size by weight is often hidden where it can't actually be seen.

Dropping from one carat to a half carat definitely doesn't mean the stone will look half as big, but the price will drop hugely. A one carat round brilliant diamond is usually about 4mm (0.16 inches) across, while a 0.5 carat stone is just over 3mm (0.12 inches).

Again I conducted an experiment - keeping the other variables the same and changing the size in 0.25 carat increments. To keep it consistent with the other experiments in this chapter, I looked at the price differences relative to a one carat stone.

Size (carat)	Price ($)	Difference ($)	Difference (%)
1.50	17.740	+8,525	+92.5
1.25	12,620	+3,405	+37.0
1.00	9,215	0	0
0.75	4,030	-5,185	-56.3
0.50	2,250	-6,965	-75.6
0.25	630	-8,585	-93.2

Again, some big results can be seen - dropping 0.25 of a carat results in a cost saving of over 50%. If we're measuring the diameter, this is a drop from 4.0mm (0.16 inches) to 3.6mm (0.14 inches).

Larger diamonds are more rare and are more likely to have noticeable inclusions, which results in the non-linear increase in price.

Dip just below

There are certain weights that are seen as landmarks – 0.5 carats, 0.75 carats, 1 carat etc. Jewellers know that these 'magic' weights are desirable, so the price of a stone that is just above them will have a premium built into it compared to one that is just underneath.

By dipping down to just below a magic weight, say to 0.98 carats instead of 1.01, you can save yourself some a noticeable amount of cash without the difference in weight being at all visible.

Metal

This might sound obvious, but a less expensive metal for the setting will leave more budget for the rock itself. Choosing white gold over platinum or reducing the karat of the gold will bring down the price you pay.

To find out just out much difference metal makes I compared different metals using a simple 4 claw solitaire setting, overleaf.

How To Buy An Engagement Ring

Metal	Price ($)	Difference ($)	Difference (%)
Platinum	980	0	0
18k white gold	765	-215	-21.9
18k yellow gold	750	-230	-23.5
14k white gold	390	-590	-60.2
14k yellow gold	370	-610	-62.2

No great surprises with the order that they come out at, but it's interesting to see how big the percentage difference actually is, especially between the gold options. And with a more complicated setting that uses more of each metal, the different in cost will be even greater.

Set and forget?

A fancy or heavy setting can add noticeably to the price of your ring. The simpler the setting, the less expensive the ring will be - there's less metal used and less craftsmanship involved. Fancier settings also often use lots of tiny gemstones to up the bling factor, which also increases the price.

To see how the setting affects price, I compared the seven most common settings on one of my recommended retailers. I kept the setting as 18k white gold and looked at just the setting, without a centre stone.

Setting	Price ($)	Difference ($)	Difference (%)
Pavé	1,975	0	0
Channel	1,925	-50	-2.5
Halo	1,650	-325	-16.5
Three Stone	1,560	-415	-21.0
Side Stone	1,340	-635	-32.2
Solitaire	750	-1,225	-62.0
Bezel	600	-1,375	-69.6

Predictably, the results show that the more bling a setting has the more expensive it is.

Pavé and channel settings both have large numbers of small diamonds on the bands and this high number of stones pushes them to the top of the table. Halo, three stone and side stone settings all make use of smaller stones supporting the centre stone, which can be a good way of increasing the impressiveness of a ring, but also adds to the cost.

We learned in chapter 4 that the ring setting was the #1 thing that women wanted to make sure was right for their rings. So, if your girlfriend has set her sights on a pavé setting, this may mean compromising on other areas of the ring - the metal used, or possibly the size of the stone to make sure that you keep within your budget.

Strength in numbers

Several smaller stones are less expensive than one large stone. For example, three diamonds at 1/3 of a carat will be much less expensive than one single solitaire that weighs 1 carat.

Fancier settings with a high number of smaller stones can actually help your budget too. Halo settings in particular, where the centrepiece is surrounded by a ring of stones, will make a small central stone look much bigger and more impressive. As with everything in this chapter, it's worth having a play with all of the different variables to see what works for you.

Buy online

As mentioned in the previous chapter, it's by buying online from retailers that have tools to allow you to dial-in your required characteristics that will allow you to save the big bucks. If 'certification' is the unofficial fifth C of buying a precious stone, then I'd like to put forward a sixth C as 'click'.

Online retailers have access to huge stocks of diamonds, which means that you can pretty much have a play with any combination of the variables and still be able to find the stone that you're looking for. You'll be able to get the exact ring that is right for you and your budget.

For the list of my recommended retailers that have the best choice, best service and best prices, navigate to www.ring-retailers.com.

Keep track of your quotes

When you're comparing different retailers and rings, it can be difficult to keep track of exactly what each ring cost and where it was that you saw it. And when you're making adjustments to the ring shape or size, it's easy to forget what it was that made the difference.

To help you keep track of all of the quotes as you compare different retailers and adjust variables on the rings, I've created a free Quote Tracker Tool which you can download from my website.

It'll be a key tool in ensuring that you get the most bling for your buck.

Check it out and download it from www.quote-tracker.com.

Real life examples

In this chapter we've looked at the different factors that affect the price of a ring affect the cost individually. To make it more tangible, I wanted to show you how combining all of these tips can give you the very best value.

The ring below could either cost you $21,230 or $8,920, despite looking pretty much exactly the same and both having a 1 carat, excellent cut diamond that will sparkle equally well. By tweaking the clarity and colour of the stone and the metal used in the ring setting, there are huge savings to be made.

Or, if you're on more of a budget, you could tweak the shape of the stone to an oval. This would drop the price even further – down to just $4,730.

Is a ring with a top quality round brilliant diamond that costs over $20k four times more impressive than the oval one? I don't think so. In fact, due to the longer shape of the oval, it will likely look larger when worn.

The actual stats of the three rings that resulted in such radically different prices are in the table below:

	Top	Middle	Lower
Stone Shape	Round brilliant	Round brilliant	Oval
Stone Size	1 carat	1 carat	1 carat
Stone Cut	Excellent	Excellent	N/A
Stone Colour	D	E	F
Stone Clarity	IF	SI1	SI1
Stone price	$20,180	$8,270	$4,550
Setting	Platinum	18k gold	14k gold

Setting Price	$1,050	$650	$180
Total Price	$21,230	$8,920	$4,730

The majority of the huge difference between top and bottom is made up of the extremely high price of the top quality round brilliant stone. But you can find big differences with any ring and stone combination.

If you wanted to up the bling factor, you could go for something like this:

As it's a halo setting, you can afford to go smaller on the central stone, without losing any impressiveness. I looked at three examples where I reduced the stone size to 0.8 carats. This brings the price down hugely for even the most expensive option.

The price varied from $11,680 for a top round brilliant stone with a platinum setting, all the down to $5,895 for a cushion cut with a 14 karat white gold setting.

Not quite such a huge disparity in price as with the solitaires, but still nearly a 50% saving with no real change in visual impact. The specs of the three options are overleaf.

	Top	Middle	Lower
Stone Shape	Round brilliant	Round brilliant	Cushion
Stone Size	0.8 carat	0.8 carat	0.8 carat
Stone Cut	Excellent	Excellent	N/A
Stone Colour	D	F	F
Stone Clarity	IF	SI1	SI1
Stone price	$7,070	$3,690	$2,550
Setting	Platinum	18k gold	14k gold
Setting Price	$4,610	$3,950	$3,350
Total Price	$11,680	$7,640	$5,900

To sum it all up

With an almost infinite number of combinations of the 4Cs and setting style it's impossible to give you a recommendation on which is the best ring to get. There is no best ring, only the best ring for you and for her.

But without getting too soppy, the engagement ring you buy is a symbol of your love, and this chapter has been all about helping you make the biggest gesture of love that you can.

Use the information to make an informed decision and make sure you get the most value you can for your budget. Have a play with all the variables and look at how they affect the price that you'll pay. Which combinations do you prefer? Which would she prefer? Spending some time testing out the different stone and setting combos will ensure you get the best ring you can for a price that you love.

15. CLOSING THE DEAL

I understand that buying online isn't for everyone, so for those who would prefer to kick it old school and buy from a shop, how can you make sure you get the most for your money and don't get the wool pulled over your eyes?

Answer: By being thoroughly prepared and by not being afraid to haggle.

Now, negotiating the Cuban missile crisis was probably pretty hard. The end of the Cold War? Quite tricky, I imagine. Knocking a bit of cash off the price of an engagement ring? It's a walk in the park.

Most people are happy to haggle on a pair of fake sunglasses from a market on holiday. The negotiation is part of the fun – and I know that my benchmark is trying to get a price close to what a local would be offered. Faith's mum grew up in Malaysia, so whenever we're over there and shopping at a market, she'll open the haggling in the local Bahasa Malay language and usually get an opening price of up to a third of what I would get. I have to work hard to get a good price, but I still enjoy the experience – haggling is expected by both parties and if it goes well we all leave happy – the mark of a good deal.

If we're happy to do it on holiday, why not back home too?

Maybe it's because of expectations of what's socially acceptable. On holiday, we know the stall holders expect it, so it becomes part of the fun. But in the sterile environment of a shopping mall, it's seen as not so much the done thing.

But you should think about rings the same way you should about cars and white goods – the price is flexible and sales people are open to negotiation. These are high-price items and the retailer needs to keep the stock moving.

Haggling is a win-win for both parties. Retailers would rather sell at a discount today than have something sit around gathering dust.

Jewellers are asked for discounts all the time. Suggesting a reduced price doesn't make you look cheap, it shows you're savvy about how you spend your money. Rich people don't stay rich by spending more than they need to.[30]

The biggest barrier to negotiation is getting over this initial fear and embarrassment. What's the worst that can happen? They say no? After you get over this, the rest can be broken down into a few simple steps, which is what I'll cover in this chapter.

Haggling is a great life skill to have in your man armoury and the following tips can be applied to buying pretty much anything. They can help in your day-to-day personal interactions too.

Remember – if you don't ask, the answer is definitely no.

Know your foe

A jeweller's main aim is to squeeze as much money as possible out of every buyer. Sure they want to help you find a great ring that will make your proposal magical, but at the end of the day they're running a business.

There are some circumstances that will make them less likely to negotiate. Make sure you don't indicate to the jeweller that any of these apply:

- You have a strong bond with a ring – if you've already decided that there's one ring to rule them all

- You're desperate - you plan to propose tomorrow but haven't bought the ring

- You're rich and an increase in the price is not important to you

- You're ill-informed about what you're looking at

How big a reduction can you expect?

The mark-up for some fine jewellery can be up to 300% but because of increased transparency in diamond prices it's more like 30-40% for a large diamond. And, as the size of the diamond increases, the lower the mark-up percentage will be.

So be realistic – although you should be able to get a discount, you won't knock 80% off the price.

Jewellery store chains have economies of scale, so while their prices may be similar to smaller jewellers, their margins should be larger. This gives you more room to negotiate.

Some luxury retailers, like Tiffany and Cartier, aren't open to negotiation. If you know your lady has her eye on a ring from a jeweller such as these, your best bet is to find a custom jeweller to recreate it. You won't get the brand name attached to it, but you can put the difference in price towards a bigger rock, an amazing honeymoon or a down payment on a jet ski.

How will it go down?

Hopefully you're convinced that haggling is worth trying so I'll explain how to go about it in four easy steps. You've already started on the first one by reading this book:

Step 1: Prepare

You may be a skilled negotiator, well-versed at hammering out corporate deals, or the guy that gets called when someone is in a bank with hostages and demanding a helicopter. But, as with all negotiations, it's the person with the most information that has the advantage. There is no weaker position in negotiations than being uninformed and indecisive.

Now, you'll never match the knowledge of someone with 25 years in the trade, but you can level the playing field by educating yourself about your intended purchase and learning some negotiating tactics.

If you go in saying you want a round 1.2 carat, G or H colour, VS1, excellent to ideal cut diamond with an 18 carat white gold Tiffany-style setting you'll put yourself in the driver's seat. You know what you're talking about and you're there to talk turkey.

If you've read this far you'll know what the above means but if you've skipped to this chapter, I'd suggest going back and reading through in more detail - blagging does not help haggling.

Step 2: Set Limits

There are two limits to think about here and both should be decided well before you get anywhere near an actual store – cost and quality.

1. Cost

This is a big question and there's no definitive answer, but before you get near a shop establish a budget. One you're in there, it's easy to succumb to price creep so have a firm budget in mind.

As we looked at in Chapter 3: Budgeting, you should be looking to buy a ring you can afford and are comfortable buying. You may need to skip a few nights out to salt away some cash for it, but it's more important to begin your life together debt-free or use the money for an amazing honeymoon.

An engagement ring is a luxury but the cost shouldn't be something you stress over.

If you can't afford the ring that you really really want, don't hold off. You can always upgrade to a nicer ring for an anniversary present later on.

2. Quality

Decide which of the four Cs are most important to you, remembering what is most important to her as well. Finding the right balance is a personal decision but by using online tools as discussed in the previous chapter you can have a play with the specs and see how they affect the price and what you should be able to get for your money.

Step 3: Stick to your limits

This is the tricky part. It's easy to get carried away when you walk in to buy a sparkly symbol of your commitment. Sales people know this and will try to push you outside your budget. A smooth-talking jeweller and can wow you with what 'just a couple of hundred more dollars' will get you and the price can creep up with ninjitsu-like stealth.

The flipside though is to make sure you go for a ring that you love. It's something that you're going to have forever, so don't accept one that isn't right.

If when shopping you struggle to find the ring you want at the price you are willing to pay, you may need to reassess one or both of your limits. But do so only from the safety of your own home and not under pressure from a salesman. Remember – impulse buys destroy lives!

Sales tactics to watch out for[31]

The 'today only' special

Adding artificial time pressure is a classic technique for closing a deal. If you're offered a great deal but want time to think, don't feel pressured to commit on the spot. If you come back the next day ready to spend, they'll still give it to you for the discounted price.

Good cop, bad cop

Not just a '70s cop show cliché. Working in a pair, one salesperson will put the hard sell on you, while the other is friendlier. The theory is that as you are befriended by the good cop you are more inclined to accept his advice. This tactic is easy to spot but surprisingly difficult to resist. The key is to be as assertive with the good cop as you are with the bad cop.

'I have to talk to my manager'

Similar to good cop, bad cop. This time the person you are speaking to is the good cop but the bad cop is hidden out the back and may not even exist. If the salesperson doesn't have the authority to close the deal, insist on talking to someone who does. If not, walk away.

Persuading you through your partner

If you involve your partner in the ring-buying process, bring her along to browse, but leave her at home when going to buy.

A common upsell tactic is to show your partner progressively more expensive rings, flattering her and increasing her expectations. It takes bravery to stick to your original budget with your wife-to-be gazing adoringly at a new, more expensive ring on her finger

Step 4: Close the deal

Good haggling is an exchange between two people trying to find a win/win deal. It shouldn't feel anything like an argument and you definitely don't need to be aggressive to be effective. In fact, if you go in trying to negotiate forcefully, it will often work against you. A cheeky request with a twinkle in your eye is the approach to take.

In life, you rarely get anything you don't ask for. If you ask nicely, and you're fair, most people will meet you in the middle.

Follow the steps below to give yourself the very best chance of getting a bargain.

1. Avoid an audience

Time your visit to avoid busy times. A salesman won't be interested in reducing his commission when they have a shop full of people who are all looking to buy. If possible, pick a quiet time like a weekday morning.

I've always found an audience makes everything more nerve-wracking, whether it's the family at a sporting event or a carful of people as I parallel park. Asking for a discount in front of people may make you feel more awkward about it. If there are lots of people about, ask if there's anywhere private you can discuss the purchase. Ideally this would be an office, but a quiet corner will do.

2. Choose your target

This is key – it's only worth starting the discussion if the person has the authority to negotiate. The part-time high school kid who only works there on Saturdays to support his Xbox habit won't be able to secure you a discount. If the person you're speaking to doesn't have the authority needed, ask to speak to someone who does.

3. Warm them up
Flat out demands for a discount won't work – a negotiation means two people working together to find a solution they are both happy with.

This is best done with a smile on your face – a few minutes of friendly chatting before you get down to business will pay dividends. If the sales person likes you, they're more likely to help you out. Your discount is at their discretion and a winning smile is harder to resist than strong-arm tactics.

4. Play it Cool
Don't let the salesperson know you've fallen in love with a particular ring. This puts the balance of power with them and gives them no incentive to come down on the price. If they don't think you're willing to walk away, you've already lost the negotiation.[32]

At the same time, you need to let them know that you're serious about doing business there and then – at the right price. You're more likely to score a deal if they know you're in a position to buy.

5. Lowball

It's vital that you get in first with your offer to set the boundaries of the negotiation. You should open with as aggressive an offer as you can – a price that would absolutely delight you, rather than just satisfy you. This is your anchor price that the sales person will counter after which, in theory, you meet somewhere in the middle.

Don't worry about your first offer being insulting. It's not – it's bold. If you don't open the negotiation the jeweller will and you will already be on the back foot.

6. Don't take no for an answer

Your offer may get flat-out rejected – the sticker price is the sticker price. But don't mistake this for the end of the negotiation – treat the 'no' as a 'not yet' and continue the discussion.

Continue the conversation by looking at other rings that do meet your price point, and asking about extras that could be included – free resizing, free polishing etc.

Asking deeper questions shows you're keen and will offer intel on the jeweller's constraints and how they might be willing to move.

7. Bring proof

If you've seen a ring for a good price, bring a print-out along to show the salesman the kind of deal you're after. They might tell you to go and purchase there, but the threat of losing out to a competitor can make people compromise.

Be prepared to hear the store's merchandise is higher quality or offers better customer service and respond by saying you'd like to buy here and now, but only for the right price.

8. Be the strong silent type

As negotiations come to a close, a classic salesman technique is staying silent. Everyone hates awkward silences and we'll do just about anything to avoid it, including negotiating against ourselves and accepting a price just to stop the awkwardness.

Your job is to make the salesman fill the silence with a cheaper offer.

If they have quoted a price, say nothing and furrow your brow to show you are, reluctantly, thinking about it. Stay quiet until they feel the need to speak again. Stay strong and this can only go one of two ways:

1. They'll repeat their offer and throw it back to you

2. They'll cave in and make a better offer

If you've been on the wrong end of this, you'll know how well it works. People make an offer and then think they've caused offence and try to fix it by adjusting the offer.

Even if you know the sales tactic, it's still difficult to counter. The golden rule to remember is: never negotiate against yourself. Don't change your offer until another has been made.

If the silence becomes unbearable and you need to break it, ask whether they have understood your offer and restate it. If you're met by nothing but stalling, you can force their hand. Directly asking them to make a new offer is better than negotiating yourself down. If you're going to give ground, make sure that they earn it.[33]

Stay strong. Stick to your guns. Get the ring for the price you want to pay.

9. Be willing to walk away

This is your trump card – unless you need to buy that day to pop the question, you can always walk away. Leaving with no deal is better than taking a bad deal. If you think the jeweller is trying to overcharge you then walking away is the ace up your sleeve.

Even this doesn't need to be the end of the negotiation. Leave the door open for the other side to change their position - leave your details and let them know what it would take to get your business.

Knowing you can walk away will give you the confidence to hold out for the deal you want.

Putting it all together

If you are planning on buying from a bricks and mortar store, this chapter is the culmination of everything you've learnt in the book so far. Once you've decided on stone, setting, band metal and everything else it's up to you to get out there and buy the thing. You should now be as prepared as you ever could be to make an informed decision and get the best ring you can with your budget.

Negotiating with a professional salesman and then throwing down a chunk of cash takes balls, but as the buyer of the ring you've probably already got those.

16. INSURANCE

You've spent time researching the ring and considerable amounts of cash buying it. Although it's boring, it's definitely a good idea to have it insured in case it gets lost or stolen. I'll keep this short, but here's a quick rundown on the options.

Choosing a policy

Finding insurance that works for you will depend on a number of things – whether you have household insurance, what your credit history is like and what budget you have left after shelling out for the ring.

A few questions to consider when choosing your policy are:

- Would the ring be covered if lost or only if it's stolen?

- How would it be replaced? With a cheque or through a jeweller specified by the insurer?

- If it's custom or vintage, how would you make sure the quality is matched?

- Is it insured for the full cost or a fraction?

- What's the excess?

- What proof would you need to make a claim?

- Are there any circumstances that aren't covered?

- Does the policy take into account what happens if your ring increases in value?[34]

Types of policy

The main policies that you will come across are:

Warranties

Not technically insurance, but your jeweller or ring manufacturer should offer a warranty against defects on their products and their work. Details may change so it's important to check what's covered.

If a part falls off due to a manufacturing defect, they should repair or replace it free of charge. But be aware that although they will re-attach a diamond to a ring if it has fallen off, it's unlikely the warranty will cover the replacement of the rock itself if a centre stone falls off and is lost.

Homeowner's/renter's insurance

Homeowner's or renter's insurance usually has an allowance for jewellery, but is subject to two caps:

1. The percentage of the policy that can cover jewellery

2. A value limit for an individual item

If your policy covers contents for $100,000, it may only cover to $10,000 worth of jewellery, with no single item allowed over $1,000.

These limits are set when you purchase the insurance, along with the excess and other details.

Standard limits are unlikely to cover the value of an engagement ring, so you'll need to get an add-on to rely on your home insurance. Submit your purchase receipt and value certification and the insurance company will adjust your policy.

Individual insurance

If you don't have a home policy, you can insure just the ring with an individual policy. Your jeweller can make recommendations or it's not hard to find a provider online.

One thing to watch out for is how policies can vary wildly between companies, so be sure to read the fine print.

Types of replacement

Insurance policies fall into three main types:

1. Replacement
2. Defined value
3. Actual value

Replacement

Replacement policies are the most common. The insurance company will replace or repair the ring using a supplier of their choice, based on the appraisal you submitted. If you list a platinum band two carat marquise diamond, they will replace it like-for-like, which means you will benefit if the price of the ring has gone up.

A disadvantage is that you are locked into using one of the insurer's preferred suppliers. If you don't like them, they may let you go elsewhere, but will only pay the price quoted by their chosen supplier. As insurance companies benefit from economies of scale, you're unlikely to get as good a deal if you go elsewhere.

Defined value
Here, you agree in advance with the company how much will be paid in case of loss.

This is done through an appraisal – sales receipts won't be accepted as evidence of value as they are not impartial. Just because you paid a certain amount, it doesn't mean it's worth that value.

If you lose the ring, the insurers will write you a cheque for the full defined value. In the case of a partial loss, say if the stone falls out and is lost, the repair or replacement will vary between policies.

Actual value
The least expensive option, an actual value policy will pay out the value of the ring less any depreciation.

If you paid $5,000 and lost it 10 years after getting hitched, the pay out may only be $4,000 to allow for wear and tear.

Read the small print

Although we click through the Ts & Cs every time we download a new version of iTunes, potentially agreeing to donate our kidneys if Apple slipped that into page 32 of 64 of the contract, with insurance it pays to read all of the conditions.

Your policy should cover every ring-threatening situation from theft to damage to dropping it down the sink. Take 10 minutes to make sure that you're protected for all eventualities and your future self will thank you.

17. CHEAT SHEET

Now we've covered everything you need to know in detail, here's a quick recap of the essential bits of info from this book, in case you want to refer to it at a later date. Over the last couple of years I've read a variety of 'how to' books and while I'm reading, I note down the most useful bits so I don't have to wade through the whole book again. Being the helpful chap that I am, I've put some together so you don't have to.

Budgeting

- Spend only what you can afford
- Don't succumb to pressure to spend more or you won't be able to enjoy the engagement
- Weddings are expensive, so make sure you start in a good financial place

What's important?

- For girls, setting is most important
- Don't get caught up in the quality of the stone
- Where you buy from and who designs it don't matter

Getting her involved

- There's no right or wrong answer– it depends on your relationship

- If you are not sure whether you should get her involved or not, you probably should

- You can keep the element of surprise and still get her involved by just buying a diamond and then choosing the setting together after the proposal

Going it alone

- Check out her existing jewellery, her clothes, her reactions to other peoples' rings. You can even check her browsing history to get hints on what she wants

- Last resort is to ask one of her friends, but choose carefully

The setting

- This is the most important factor when choosing a ring. If you get your girl's opinion on one thing, make it the setting.

Picking the band

- Match the colour to her favourite jewellery

- It's basically a toss-up between gold or 'white' coloured

Sizing

- Find an existing ring and go from there
- Average ring size is US 6, UK L ½
- If in doubt, go larger as it is easier to resize down

Diamonds

- Don't skimp on cut – get the best you can afford
- You can economise on clarity – down to SI1 is safe and will be 'eye-clean'

Other stones

- Other gems can work but need to be looked after more carefully
- Rubies, sapphires and emeralds will have all been treated
- A bezel setting will offer protection for the stone

Where to buy

- Online offers the best prices and choice
- Buy only from well-established businesses that specialise in diamonds
- Make sure you can get proper certification

Making your money go further

- Less fashionable cuts are better value –

cushion, asscher and emerald shapes are much less expensive than a round brilliant cut

- Again, don't obsess over clarity – anything down to SI1 will appear perfect to the naked eye
- Dip just below a whole carat to get a good deal
- Have a play with the different variables to see what works for you

Closing the deal

- Decide on your limits before you go near a jewellery store
- Go at a quiet time and only talk to someone with the authority to give a discount
- Don't be afraid to haggle – jewellers are used to it
- Lowball
- Stay strong and silent – don't crack under the pressure
- Don't be afraid to walk away
- Do it all with a smile on your face

Insurance

- Adding it to your household insurance is the best value
- Read the fine print
- Ensure it covers the ring if it is lost as well as stolen

- Sales receipts don't count as evidence of value – you need an independent certificate
- Check the replacement type – direct replacement, defined value or actual value. Make sure you are happy with it.

18. HOW I DID

At the start of the book, I started to tell you about my miserable proposal opportunity that went awry on top of a Hawaiian volcano. There was supposed to be beautiful sunrise and majestically-bosomed native girls parading around and yet there we were cold, wet and huddling under a stolen blanket.

You probably guessed that there was a happy ending though.

After deciding to call it a day, we trudged back towards the car park, looking forward to a nice cup of tea to brighten up our morning. Then suddenly the clouds cleared. Golden rays of light shone through and we were treated to a sunrise worthy of an instagram #unfiltered hashtag. "This is it!" I thought and took a deep breath. I dropped to one knee and pulled out the ring box. In my excitement I snapped the lid completely off it, but soldiered on and popped the question.

Faith burst into tears, but through the snotty blubs I could just about make out a yes, which was good enough for me. I must have got some dust in my eye and I am pretty sure that someone was pickling onions nearby because my eyes began to leak a little bit too.

The ring was jammed on her finger, pics taken for the required Facebook update and the deal was done.

My purchasing process

As I've mentioned, I had listened for hints on what sort of engagement ring Faith wanted, so knew exactly what I was looking for.

I had no preconceived notions of where to buy the ring, so to start I visited local jewellers, spoke to a friend of a friend who is a custom jeweller and looked extensively online.

The more research I did into what really mattered and made a difference to an engagement ring, the clearer it became that jewellery stores couldn't match the choice available online.

They were limited in stock and I didn't enjoy having to ask sales staff for the details of every ring I looked at. Showing any interest was a red flag of encouragement for the sales staff. After telling a few I'd have a think and come back, I decided that unless I was going into a store to actually buy that day, it wasn't worth researching in person.

The custom jeweller could give me anything I wanted, but this was almost too much choice. I didn't feel I had enough knowledge, or taste, to design my own ring without it going horribly wrong. They could help me find a custom ring to my required specs, but I'd be paying a premium for a custom service and not using it to its full potential.

Online offered great prices and unlimited choice and by being smart about how I chose my diamond and using the online tools to dial-in the specs to what I was looking for, I found that I could save big and still get a fantastic ring.

The ring

I eventually bought the ring from one of my recommended retailers in the UK when I was back from Australia visiting family.

I knew I was going to reduce the clarity to a level where it would appear perfect to the naked eye but give me a much lower price. In end I went with VS2 clarity - just a notch above SI1 - to make doubly sure that no inclusions would be visible.

I chose an Asscher cut because it offers great value while being a classic and classy shape.

Size-wise I dipped just below 1 carat, to take advantage of the drop in price below this 'magic weight'.

And I went for a 18 karat white gold solitaire setting - nice and simple and it shows off the stone perfectly.

I made sure that the retailer had a solid return policy in case the ring wasn't what I was expecting, but I shouldn't have worried - it was perfect.

I know if that I hadn't done my research, I would have spent more and ended up with a smaller ring. Although it may have had a higher clarity rating and technically have been higher quality, it would have looked less impressive.

The result

Faith loved her ring – it was exactly what she had pictured and drew lots of admiring comments. Girls get competitive when they compare rings and I'm pleased to say that hers easily holds its own.

Buying the ring was a great result for me too. I had a brand new fiancée and I had managed to get a more impressive ring than my friends, while spending less money.

Win-win all round!

Thank you and good luck with the search!

Thanks for buying and reading this book – I've enjoyed writing it and hope that it will help you on your search. I know I would have appreciated it when I was looking. Hopefully it helps you get the ring that your ladyfriend wants at a price that you love.

After reading this book buying an engagement ring shouldn't be a daunting process any longer, but you've still got the nerve-racking asking of the question itself to look forward to, so best of luck with that too!

Cheers,

Alastair

19. RESOURCES ROUND-UP

Throughout the book I've mentioned a few of pages on my website with free tools that will help you with your ring hunt. I've included them again here so that you don't have to go back through and find the links when you want to check them out.

Recommended Retailers

A list of trusted online retailers which all offer you the ability to tailor all aspects of the ring to make sure that you're getting exactly what you want.

If you're looking for the best choice, the best service and the best prices these are the ones to go with.

Find my recommended retailers by navigating to:

www.ring-retailers.com.

Ring Quote Tracker

A downloadable tool that will be invaluable in helping you keep track of rings with different specs and from different retailers, as well as recording the link for each ring if you're looking online.

Download the tracker at www.quote-tracker.com.

Ring Measurer

An essential print-out guide to help you find the right size for your lady's finger.

There are two ways to go about finding the correct size: either by measuring her finger if you're getting her involved in the purchasing process, or by measuring one of her existing rings and using that to determine the ring finger size.

Find the tool at www.ring-measurer.com.

RING SIZE TABLE

Inside diameter		Inside circumference		Sizes			
(in)	(mm)	(in)		USA & Canada	UK & ANZ	BRIC	EU
0.586	14.88	1.84	46.8	4	H	7	6.75
0.594	15.09	1.87	47.4	4¼	H½		7.5
0.602	15.29	1.89	48	4½	I	8	8
0.61	15.49	1.92	48.7	4¾	J		8.75
0.618	15.7	1.94	49.3	5	J½	9	9.25
0.626	15.9	1.97	50	5¼	K		10
0.634	16.1	1.99	50.6	5½	K½	10	10.5
0.642	16.31	2.02	51.2	5¾	L		11.25
0.65	16.51	2.04	51.9	6	L½	11	11.75
0.658	16.71	2.07	52.5	6¼	M	12	12.5
0.666	16.92	2.09	53.1	6½	M½	13	13.25
0.674	17.12	2.12	53.8	6¾	N		13.75
0.682	17.32	2.14	54.4	7	N½	14	14.5

Alastair Smith

Inside diameter		Inside circumference		Sizes			
(in)	(mm)	(in)		USA & Canada	UK & ANZ	BRIC	EU
0.69	17.53	2.17	55.1	7¼	O		15
0.698	17.73	2.19	55.7	7½	O½	15	15.75
0.706	17.93	2.22	56.3	7¾	P		16.25
0.714	18.14	2.24	57	8	P½	16	17
0.722	18.34	2.27	57.6	8¼	Q		17.5
0.73	18.54	2.29	58.3	8½	Q½	17	18.25
0.738	18.75	2.32	58.9	8¾	R		19
0.746	18.95	2.34	59.5	9	R½	18	19.5
0.754	19.15	2.37	60.2	9¼	S		20.25
0.762	19.35	2.39	60.8	9½	S½	19	20.75
0.77	19.56	2.42	61.4	9¾	T		21.5
0.778	19.76	2.44	62.1	10	T½	20	22
0.786	19.96	2.47	62.7	10¼	U	21	22.75
0.794	20.17	2.49	63.4	10½	U½	22	23.25
0.802	20.37	2.52	64	10¾	V		24
0.81	20.57	2.54	64.6	11	V½	23	24.75

REFERENCES

1.
http://www.kitco.com/ind/Zimnisky/2013-06-06-A-Diamond-Market-No-Longer-Controlled-By-De-Beers.html

2.
http://www.nytimes.com/2013/05/05/fashion/weddings/how-americans-learned-to-love-diamonds.html?pagewanted=2&_r=2&adxnnl=1&adxnnlx=1386289031-Mczgpl4Kvs9TLYjcrFXCZw

3.
http://www.coca-colacompany.com/holidays/the-true-history-of-the-modern-day-santa-claus

4.
http://jobsearch.about.com/od/glossary-a/a/average-salary.htm

5.
http://www.glamour.com/weddings/blogs/save-the-date/2013/09/for-once-and-for-all-how-much.html

6.
http://www.youtube.com/watch?v=lAl28d6tbko

7.
http://theknotb2b.files.wordpress.com/2013/01/
rjo-2013-more-customers-more-sales.pdf

8.
http://www.brainyquote.com/quotes/quotes/b/
benjaminfr162078.html

9.
http://www.fleur-de-coin.com/articles/oldest-
coin

10.
http://www.moneymuseum.com/moneymuseu
m/library/pictures/image.jsp?lang=en&ix=2&i=6

11.
http://www.gold.org/investment/why_and_ho
w/faqs/#q021

12.
http://curiosity.discovery.com/question/america
-produce-trash

13.
https://www.mygemologist.com/learn/jewelry-
metals/white-gold-and-platinum-differences

14.
http://www.celtarts.com/ring_size.htm

15.
http://www.bluenile.com/au/diamonds/diamo
nd-cut

16.
http://www.adiamondbuyingguide.com/pear_sh
aped_diamonds.html

17.
Saul Spero, Diamonds, Love, and Compatibility:
So You Think You'Ve Got a Gem, Exposition Pr of
Florida (July 1977)

18.
http://www.bbc.co.uk/news/business-24934297

19.
http://www.kimberleyprocess.com/en/faq

20.
http://archive.lewrockwell.com/orig11/ryan-
k1.1.1.html

21.
http://www.kimberleyprocess.com/en/about

22.
http://www.minsocam.org/msa/collectors_corne
r/article/mohs.htm

23.
http://www.farlang.com/gemstones/smith-diamonds-pearls-stones/tmp65-23

24.
http://www.gemnation.com/base?processor=getPage&pageName=sapphire_understanding

25.
http://www.ebay.com/gds/Comprehensive-Guide-to-buying-Rubies-/10000000001079961/g.html

26.
http://www.gia.edu/emerald-quality-factor

27.
http://www.ebay.com/gds/Emerald-Quick-Reference-Buying-Guide-/10000000000720069/g.html

28.
http://daughterofhypatia.blogspot.com.au/2011/03/like-black-diamonds-youve-been.html

29.
http://www.diamondreview.com/tutorials/jewelers-local

30.

http://www.familycircle.com/family-fun/money/how-to-bargain/?page=4

31.
http://www.diamondreview.com/tutorials/diamond-negotiating

32.
How To Haggle: Professional Tricks For Saving Money On Just About Anything – Max Edison

33.
http://www.artofmanliness.com/2011/05/11/how-to-haggle-like-your-old-man

34.
http://theknot.ninemsn.com.au/engagement/engagement-rings-engagement/insurance-101-engagement-ring-insurance